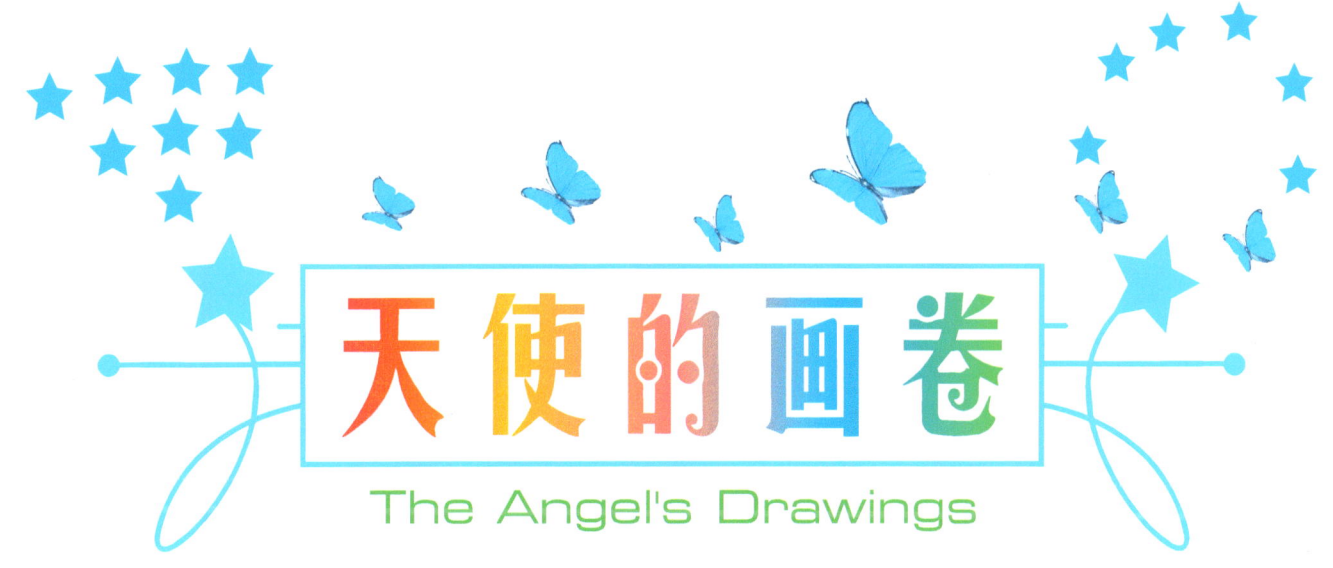

天使的画卷

The Angel's Drawings

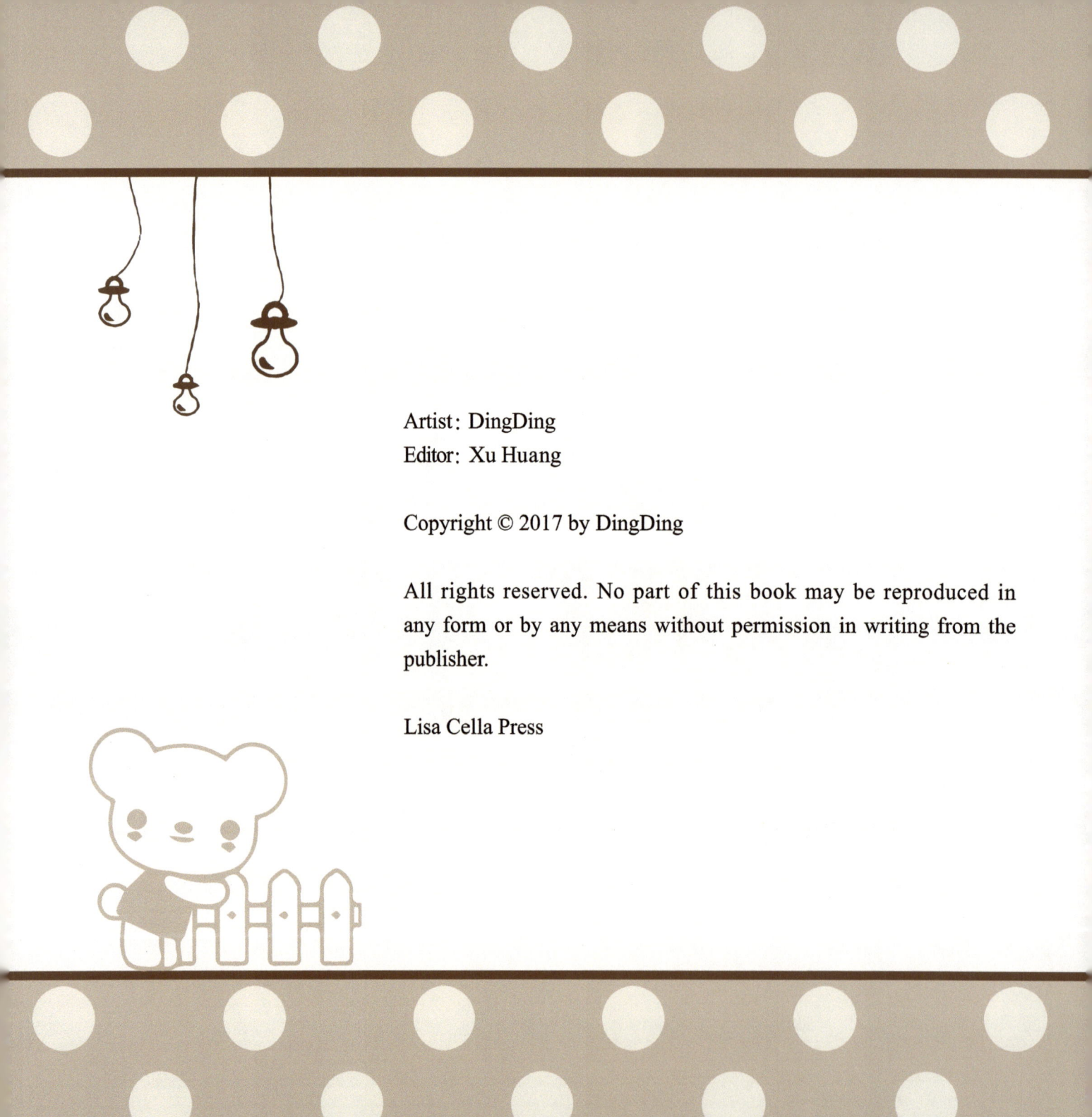

Artist: DingDing
Editor: Xu Huang

Lisa Cella Press

献给所有关心丁丁成长的人！

Dedicated to all caring for the growth of Ding Ding !

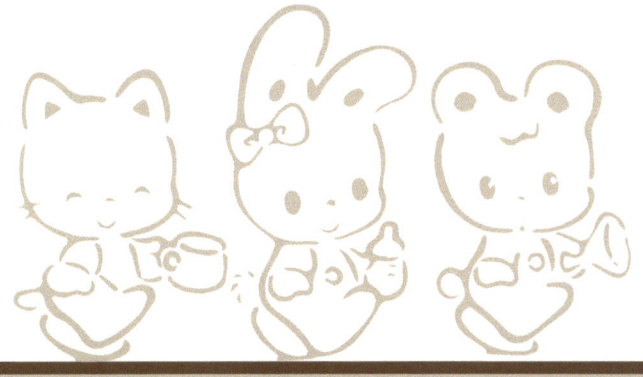

每个孩子都是天才

（代序）

丁丁从小爱拿笔画画，刚开始，我和爸爸以为乱涂乱画，一问之下，她都能向我们解释画的东西是什么，有什么含义，这让我们惊奇，同时也让我们意识到，小娃娃也有自己的思想，自己的世界。后来，她画的画越来越多，我就想把这些画收藏起来，作为她成长的纪念。

这些画都是丁丁上小学之前画的。标题是出版的时候，根据她的解释，我们一起商定的。她酷爱看动画片《米奇妙妙屋》，给自己起名叫米奇。她画的画，很多是米奇和妈妈米妮、爸爸高飞的快乐生活。除此之外，还有与小动物、各种植物以及蓝天、白云、雪花等大自然和谐相处的景象。孩子的画，没有任何技巧，却是最真的表达，直抵人心，让人感动，甚至震撼。丁丁如此，我相信所有的孩子都如此。出版她的画，具有超越纪念的意义——我想告诉所有的父母，每个孩子都是天才，给孩子一个空间，让她／他自由飞翔吧，她／他一定会给你大大惊喜！

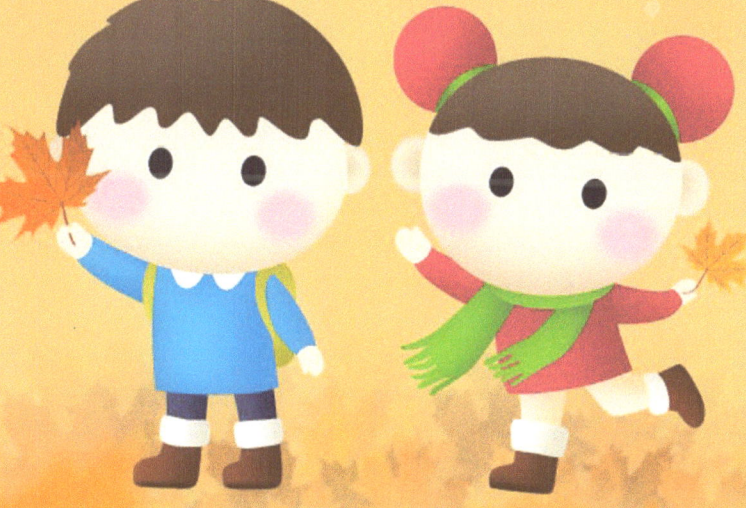

以此献给所有的小朋友和父母们！

丁丁妈妈

2017 年 1 月 6 日

Every Child Is a Genius

DingDing has been enjoyed drawing since a baby. We thought these graffiti were random. Then we learned from her that every drawing meant something, which surprised us. This made us to realize that such a baby has their own thinking and world. While she produced more and more drawings, I started to collect them as her footprints of her growth.

All these drawings are made before DingDing's elementary school. The titles are created after "consulting" her about the meaning of each painting. She loves the cartoon character Mickey so she named herself Mickey. Many of her drawings are about the happy life of Mickey's family. Besides little animals, plants, blue sky, white clouds, snowflakes are elements of her drawings. With basic drawing skills, she expresses her rich feelings reaching from her heart to the viewers' heart. The purpose of publishing DingDing's painting is to tell all parents that every child is a genius. Give their enough space to fly and they will return you a big and good surprise.

To all children and parents.

DingDing's mom
January 6, 2017

Contents

第一部分 涂鸦

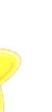

Chapter One: Graffiti

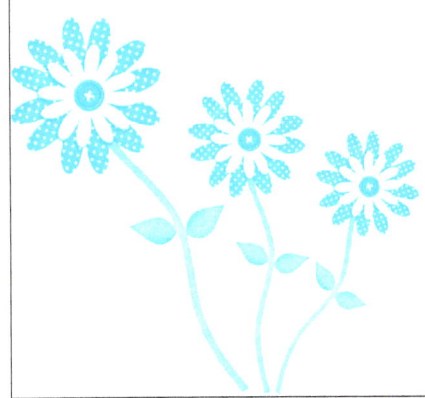

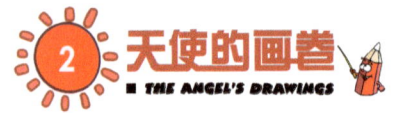

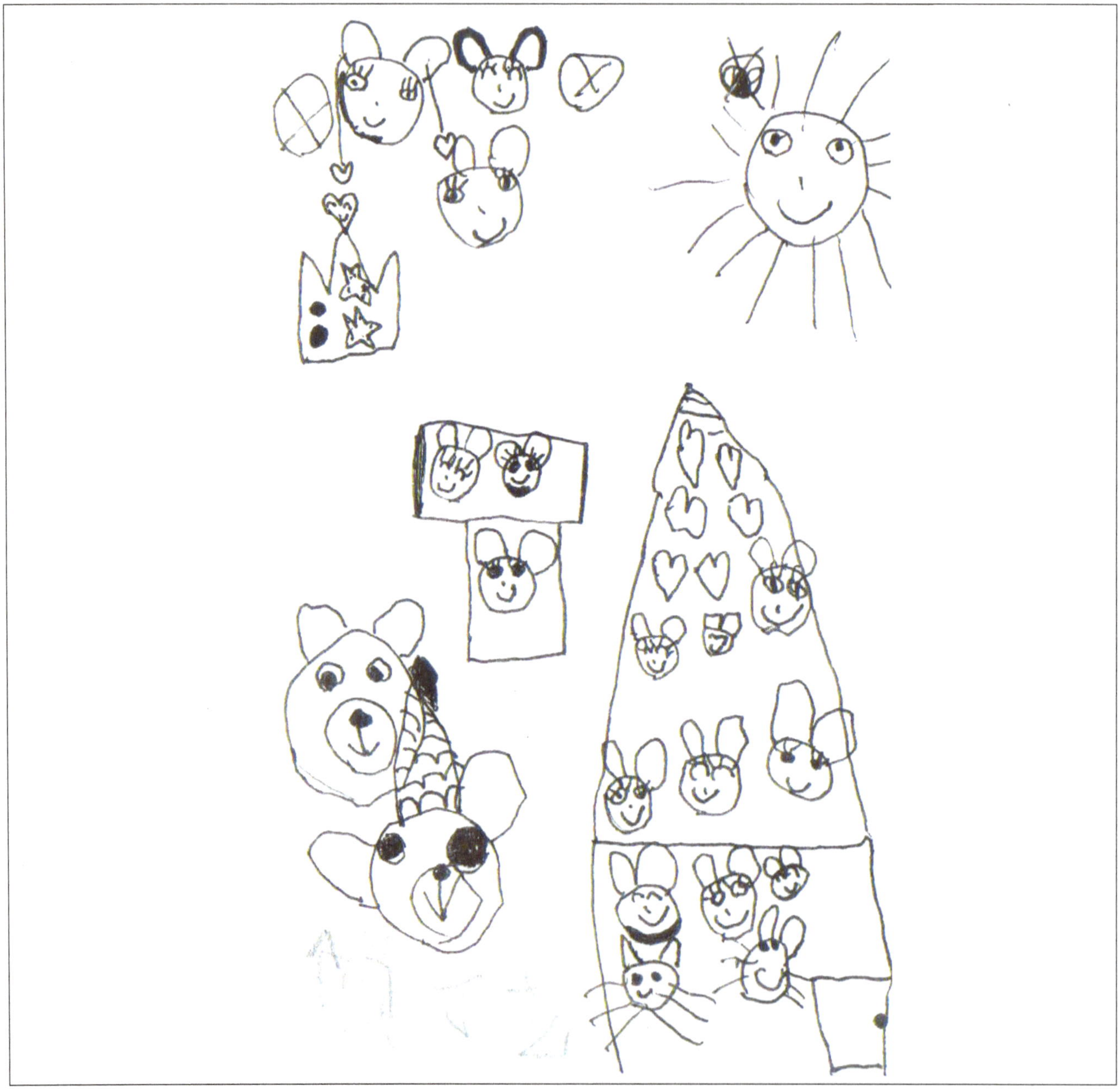

米奇和小动物们（Mickey and his friends）

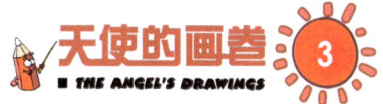

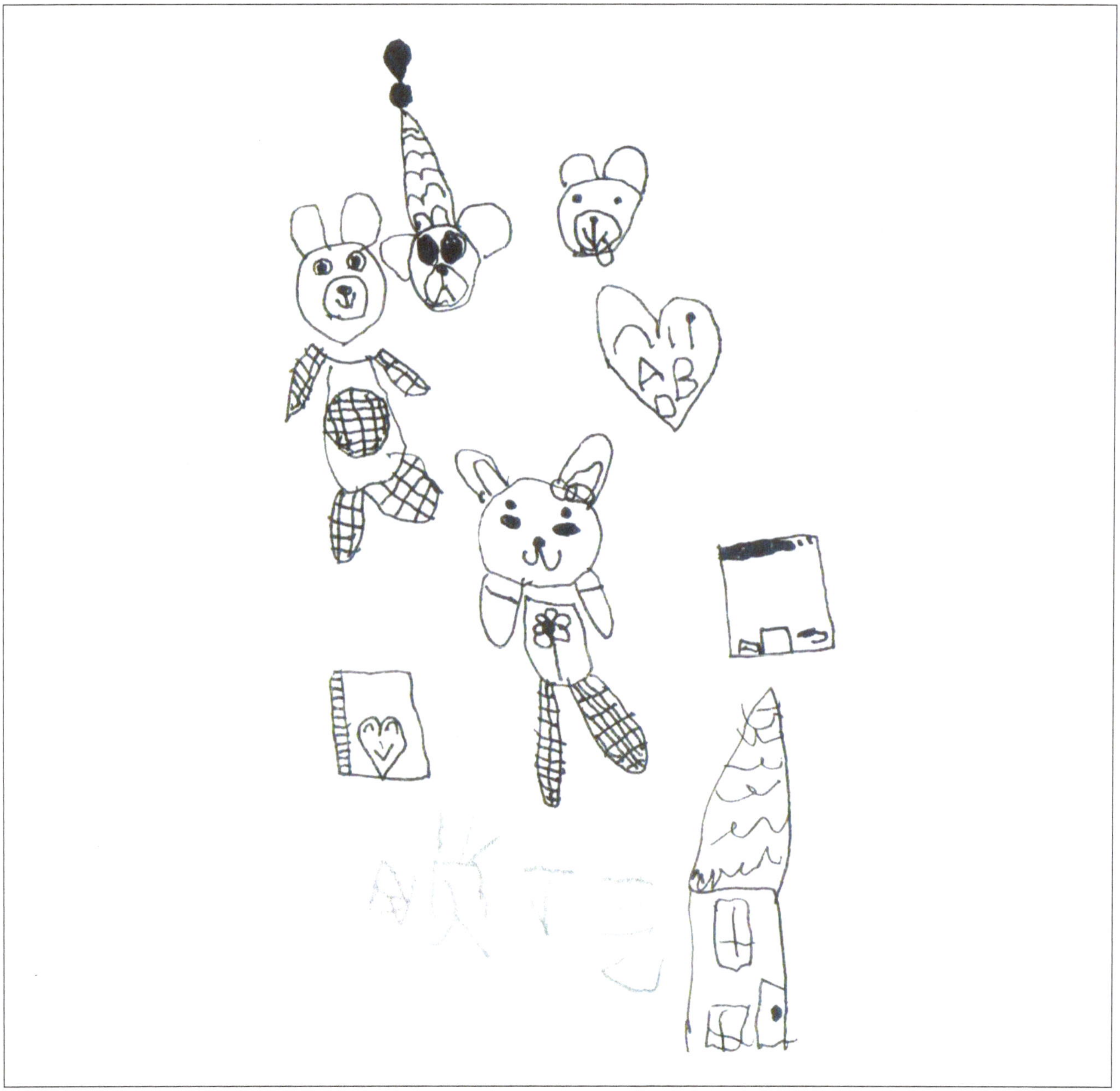

小熊和小兔子（Teddy and Bunny）

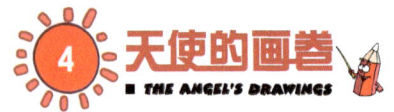
米奇、米妮、高飞一家人的快乐生活（Happy family life of Mickey, Minnie and Goofy）

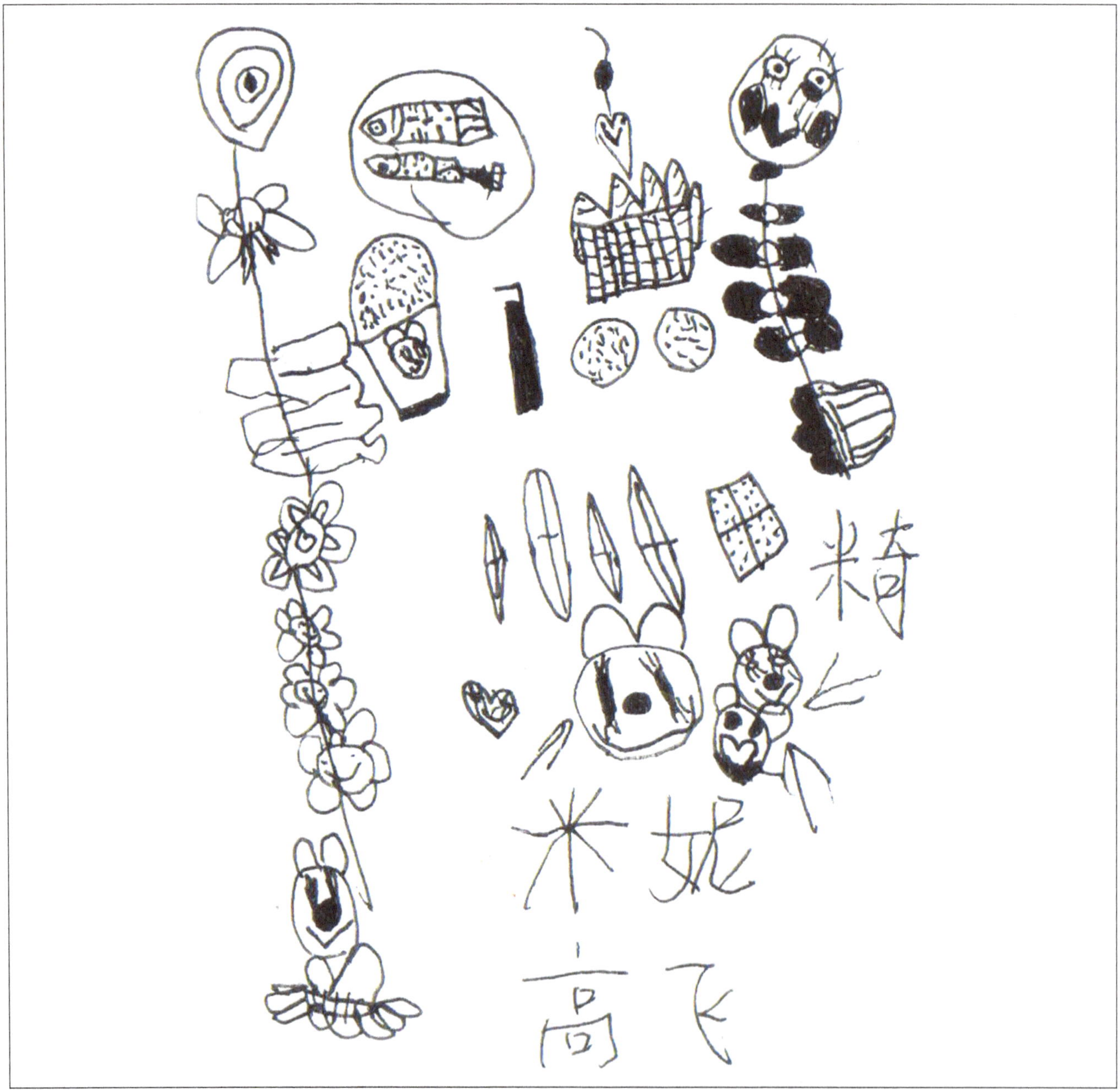

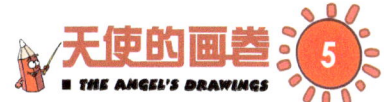

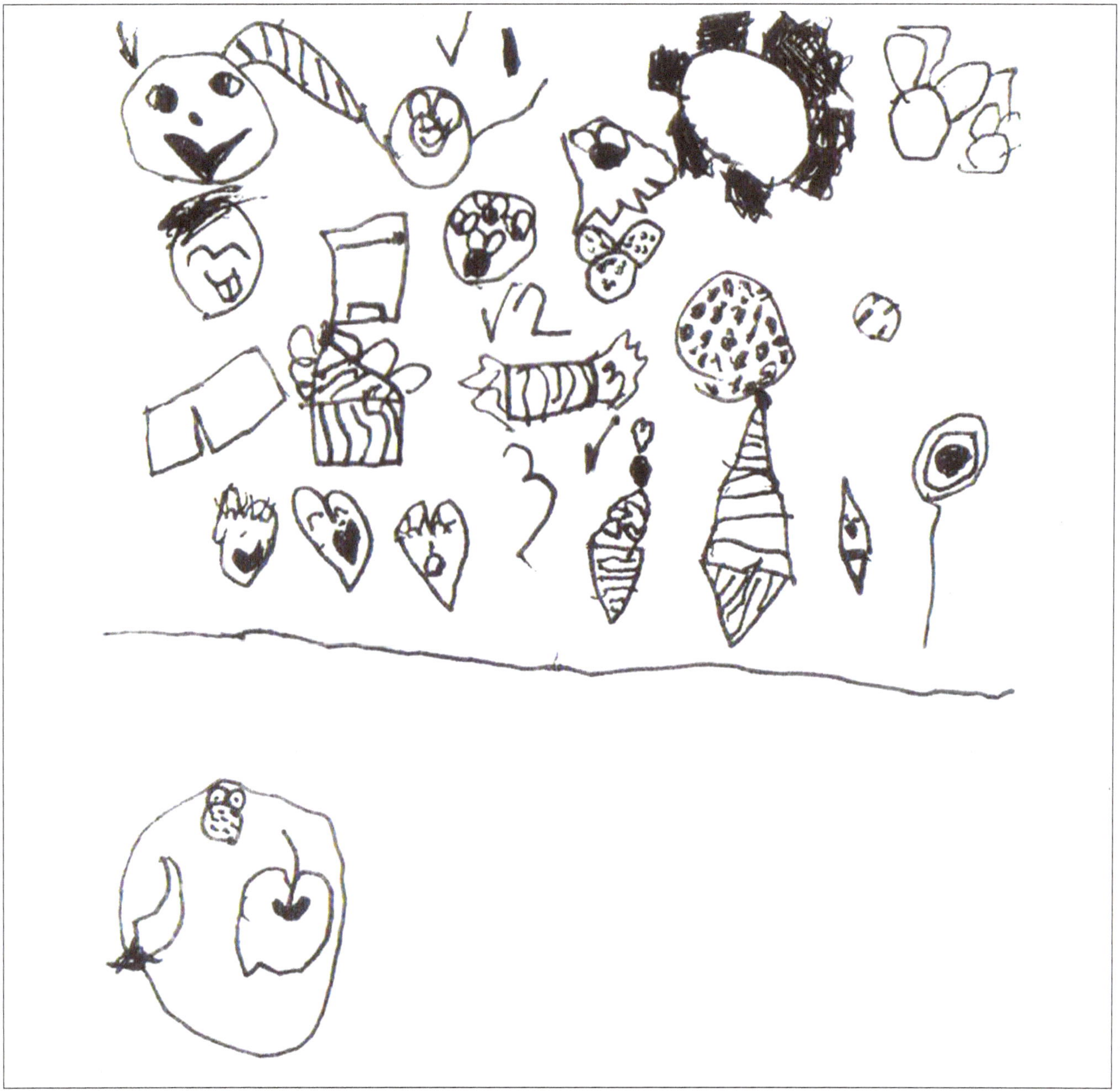

米奇的美食（Mickey's favorite foods）

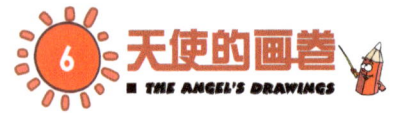

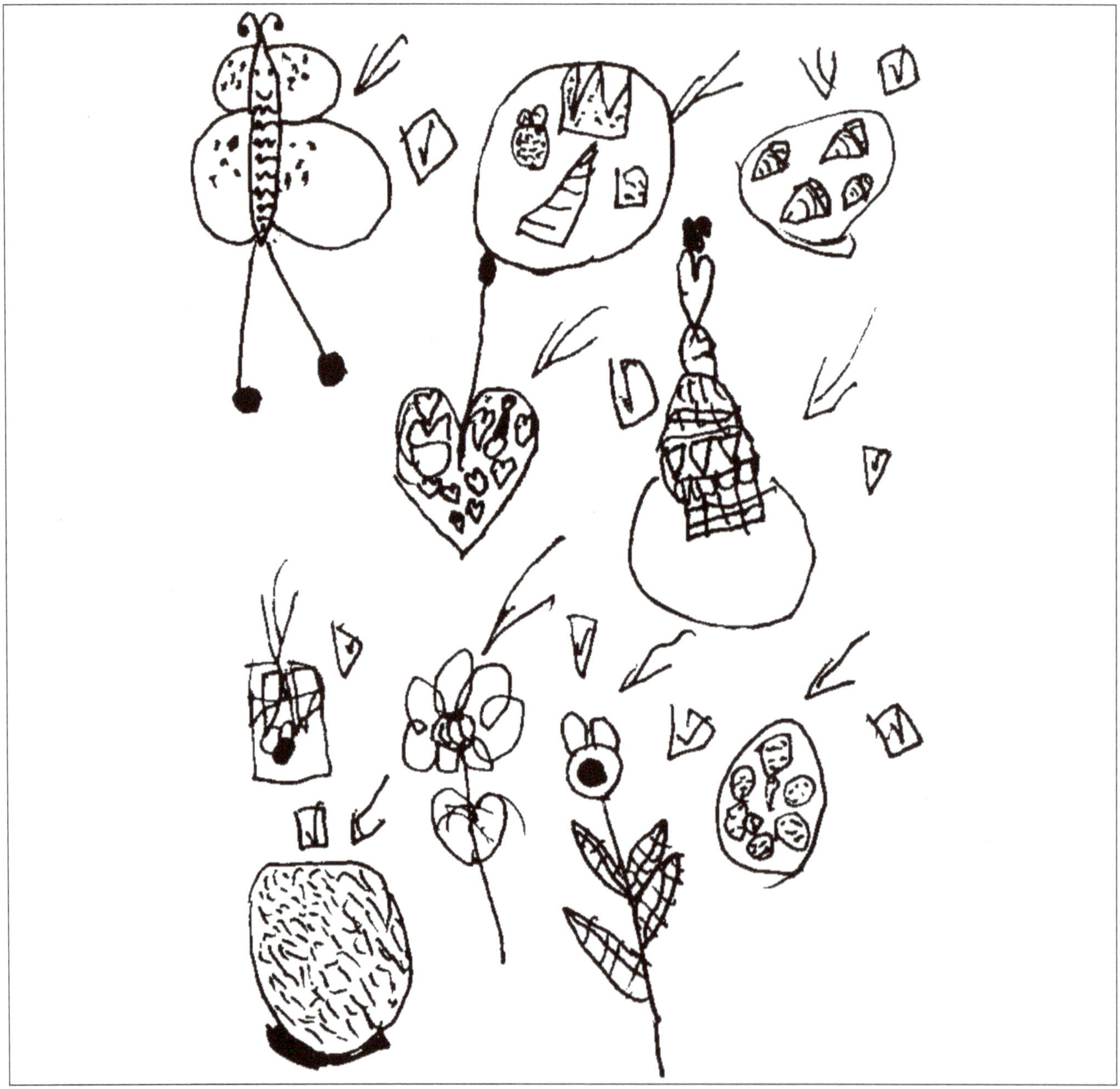

蝴蝶的美食（Butterfly's favorite foods）

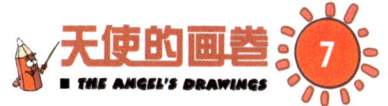

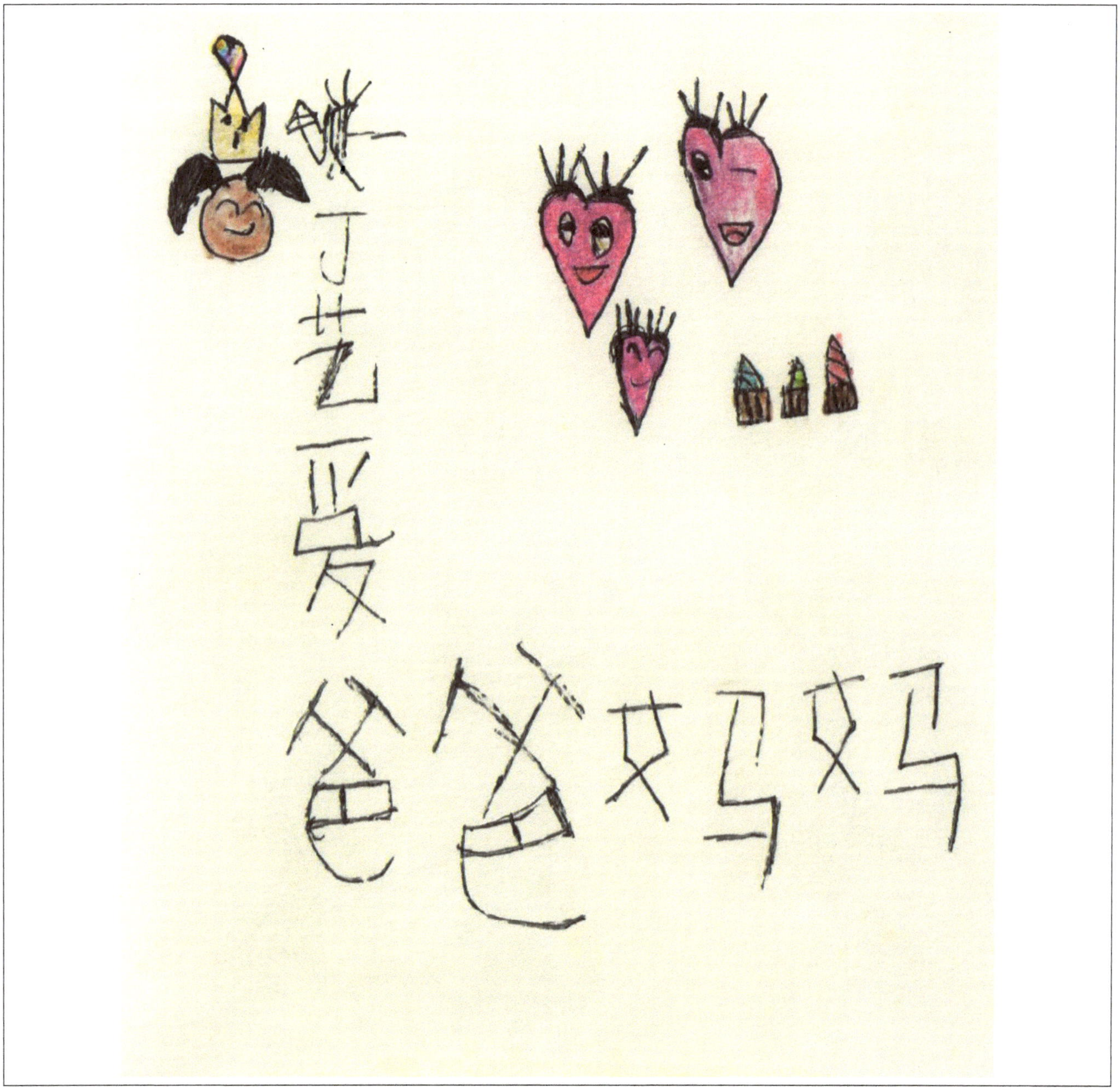

丁丁爱爸爸妈妈（DingDing Loves daddy and mommy）

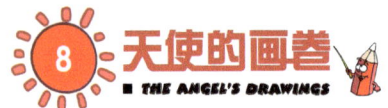

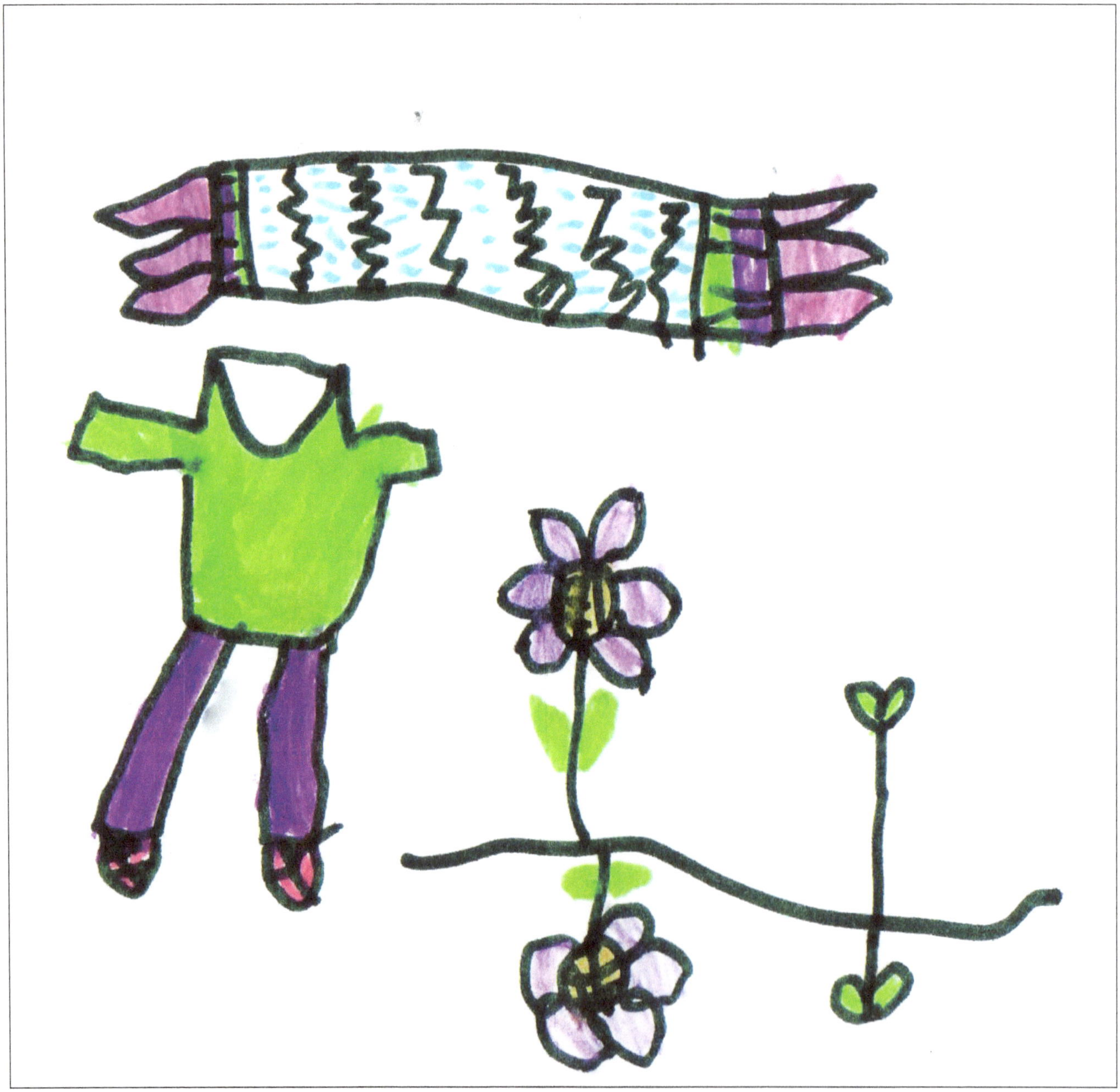

衣服和河边的小花（Cloths and the flowers on river bank）

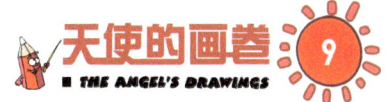

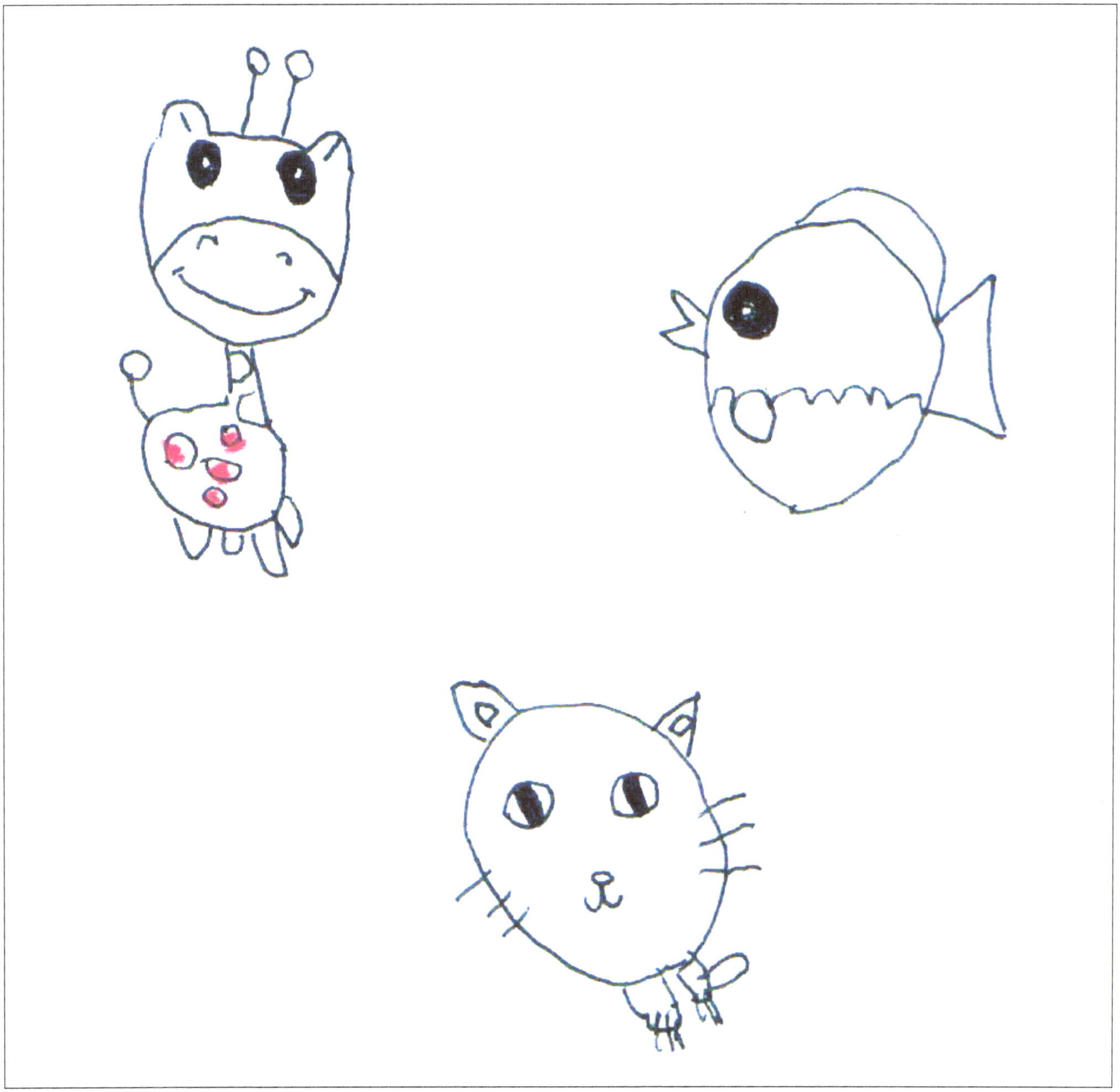

长颈鹿、小鱼和猫咪（A giraffe, a little fish and a catty）

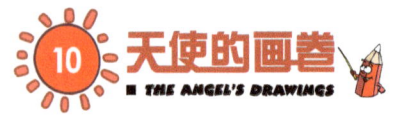

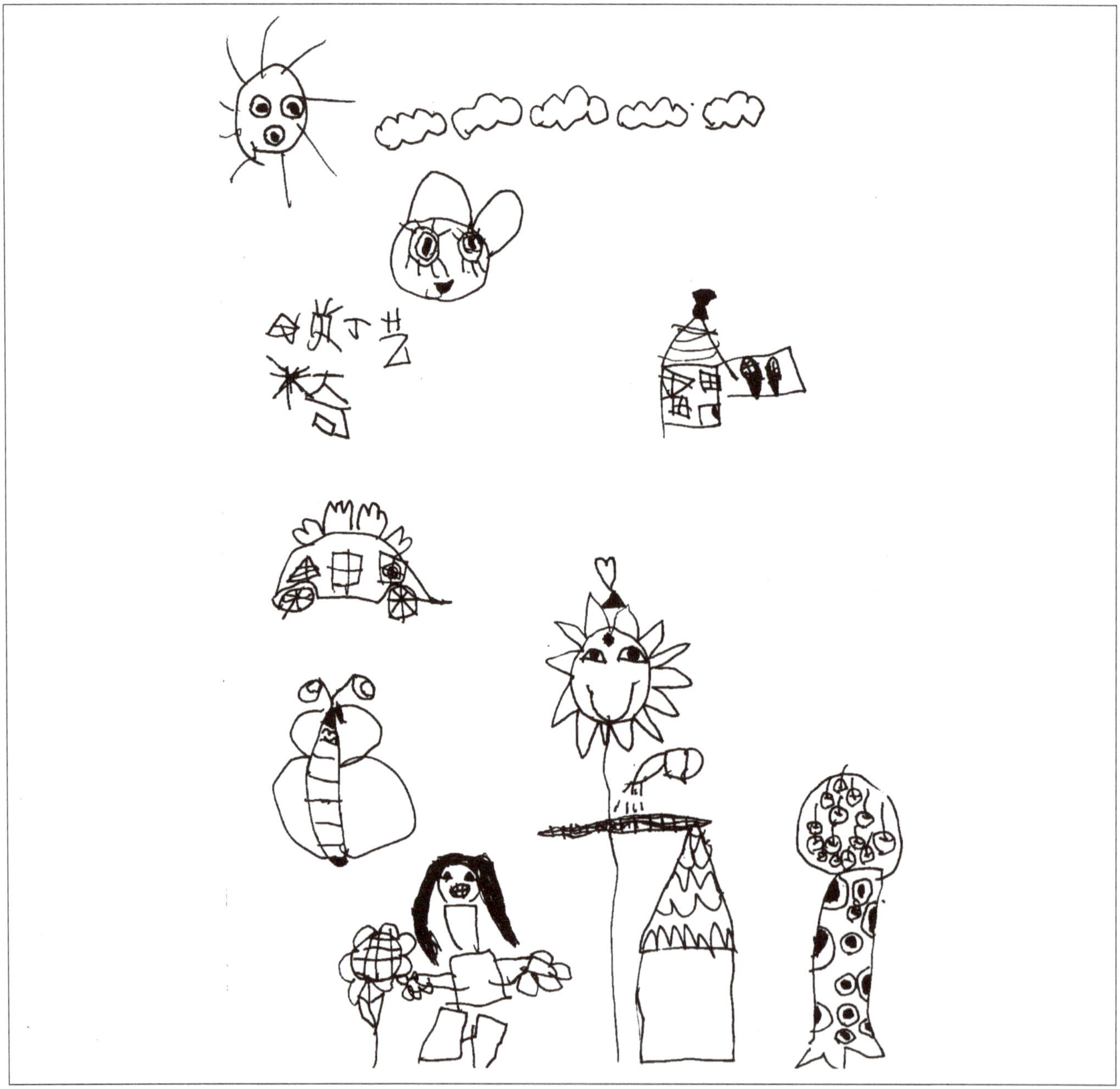

米奇的乐园（Mickey's play yard）

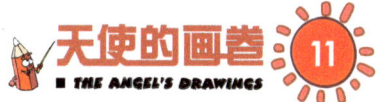

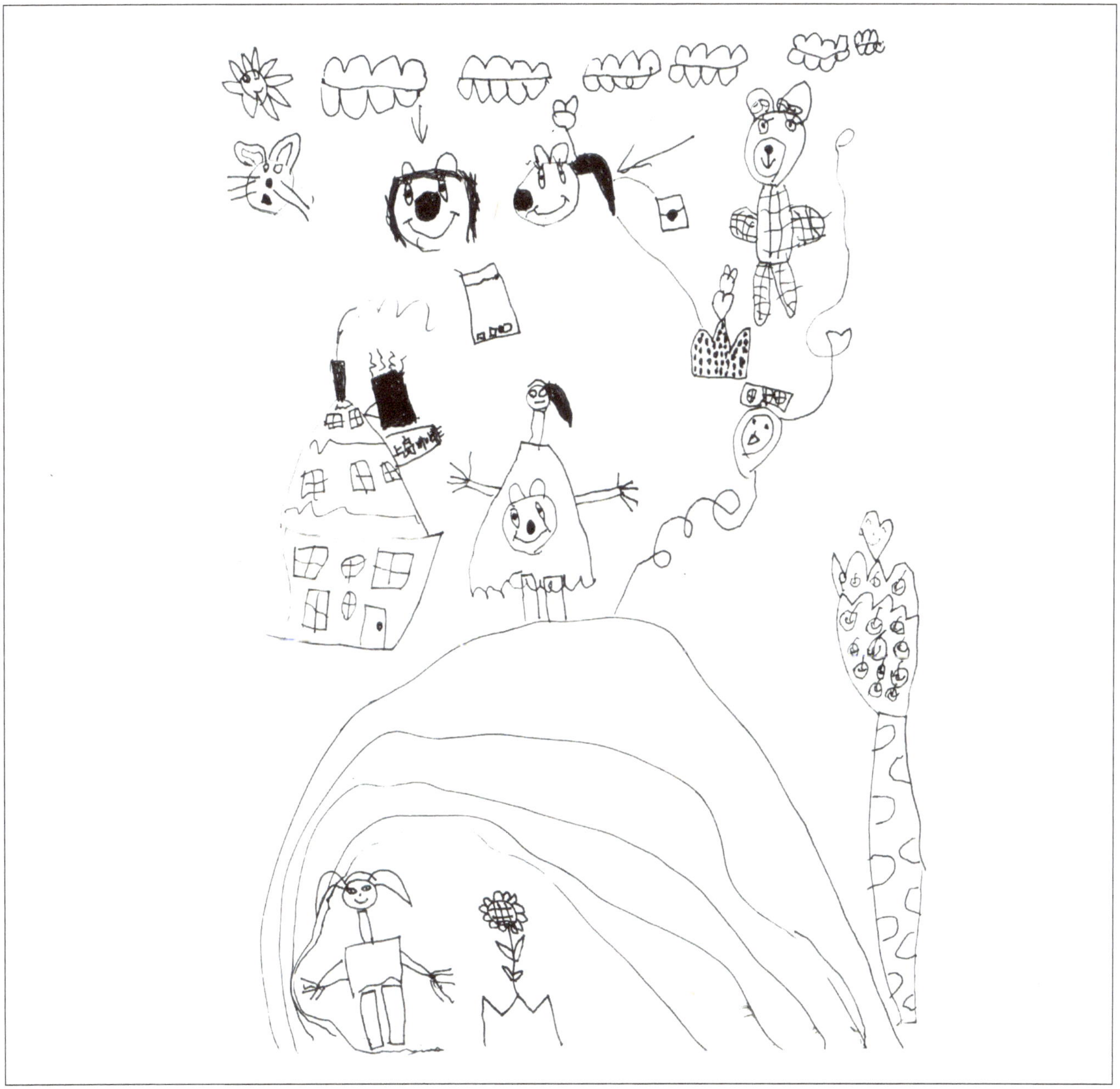

米奇最爱的彩虹季节（Mickey's favorite rainbow season）

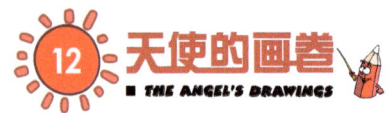

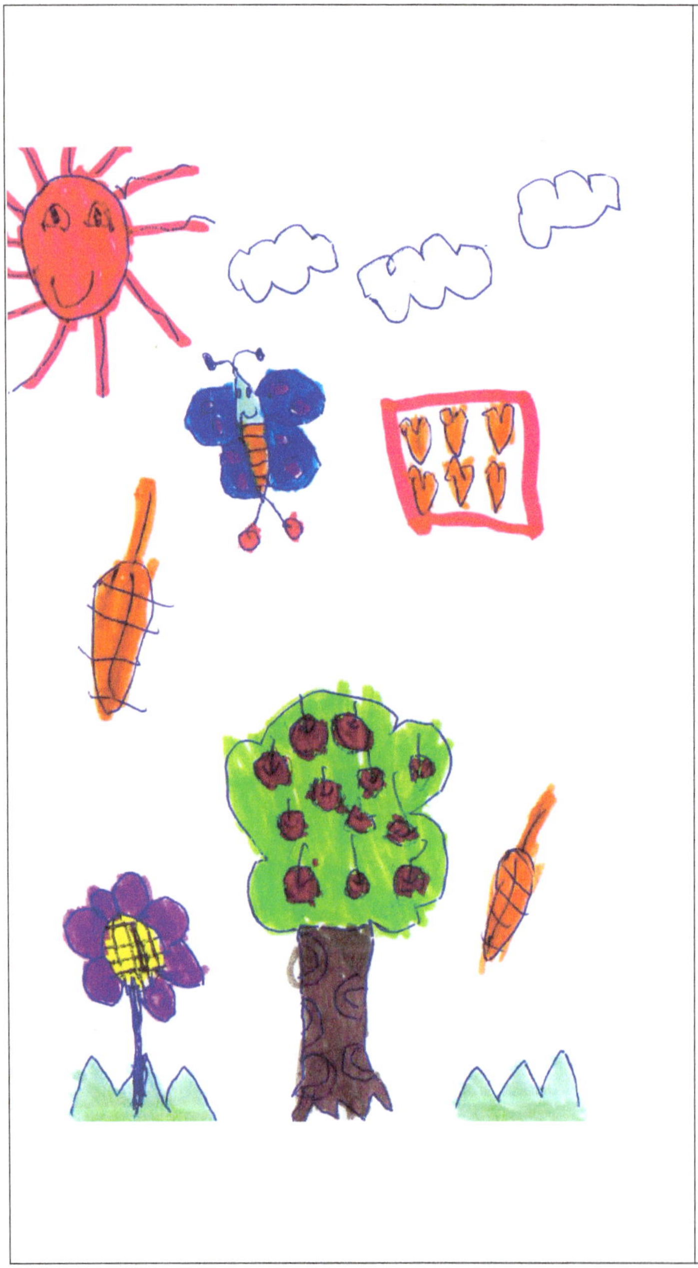

收获的季节（Season of the harvest）

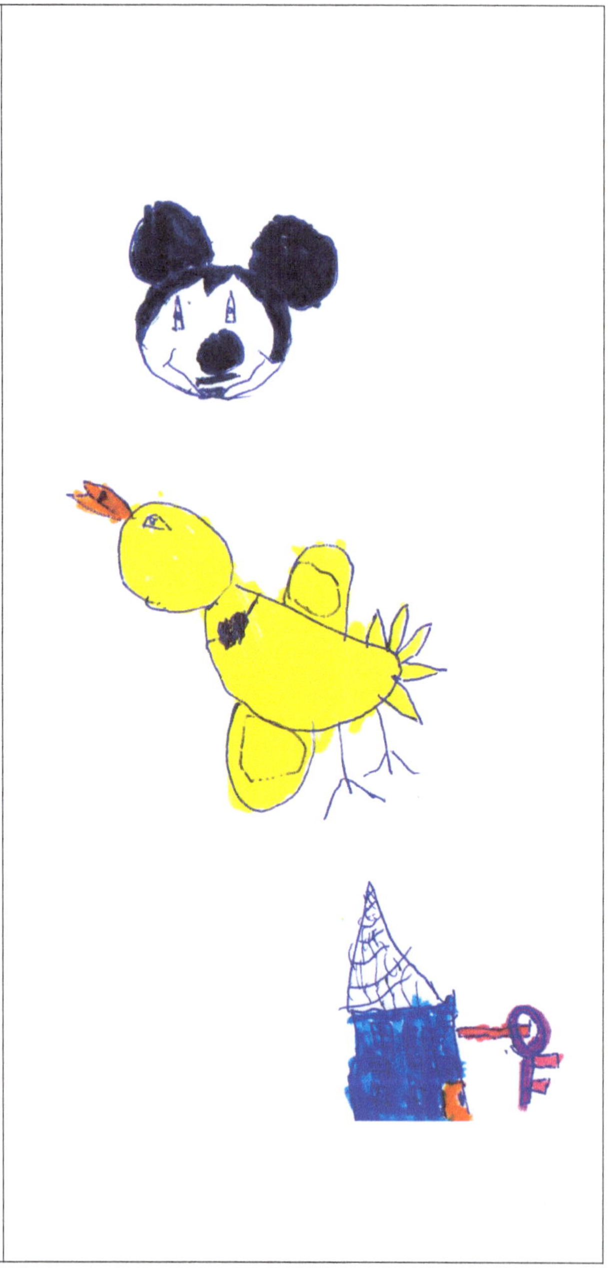

米奇的家（Mickey's home）

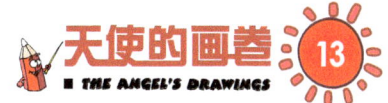

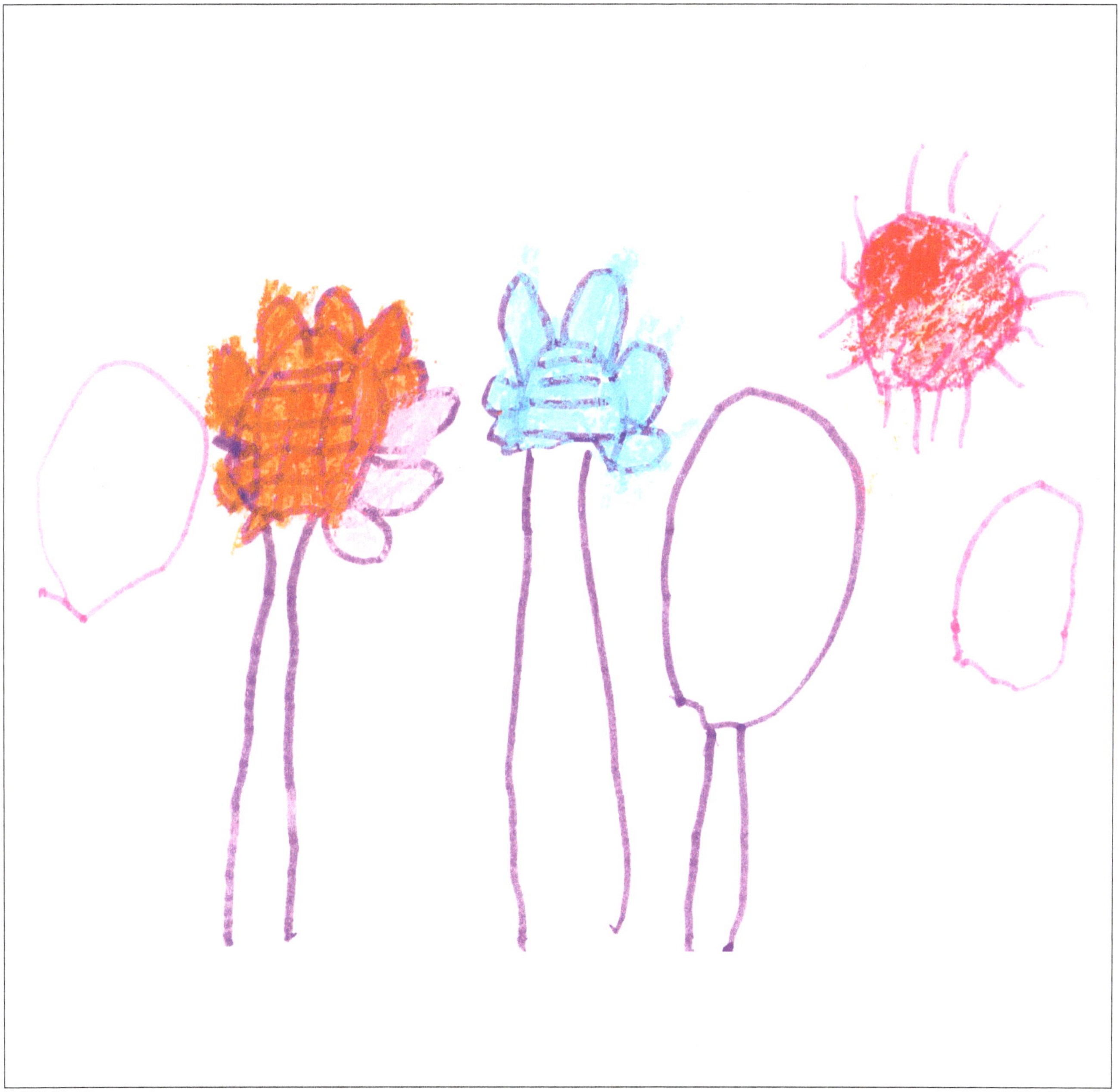

向日葵（Sunflowers）

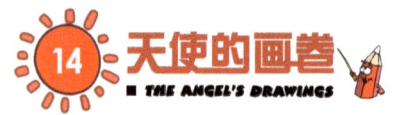

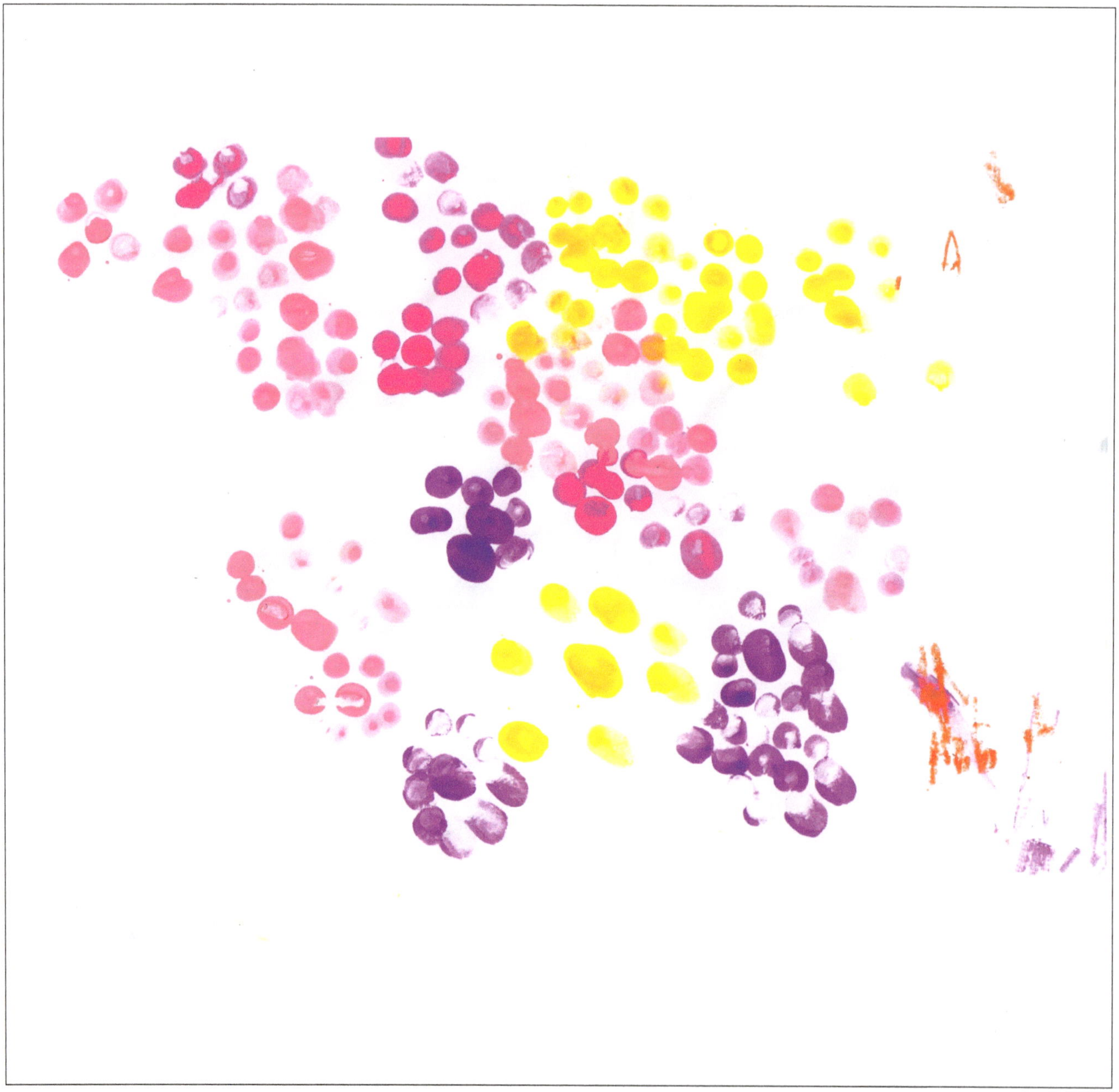

花儿（Flowers）

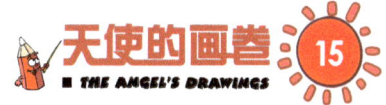
五彩的花（Colorful flowers）

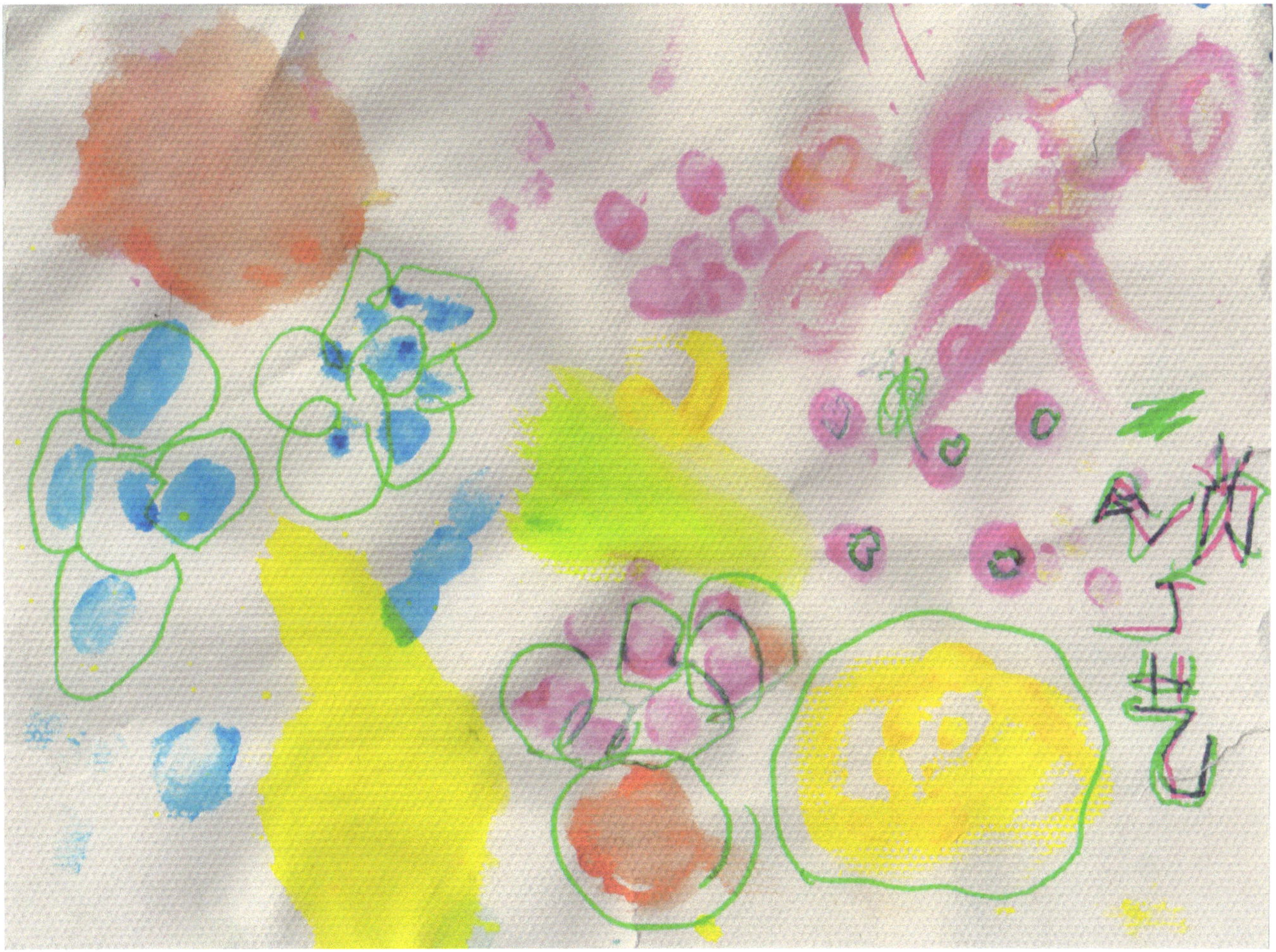

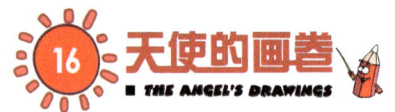

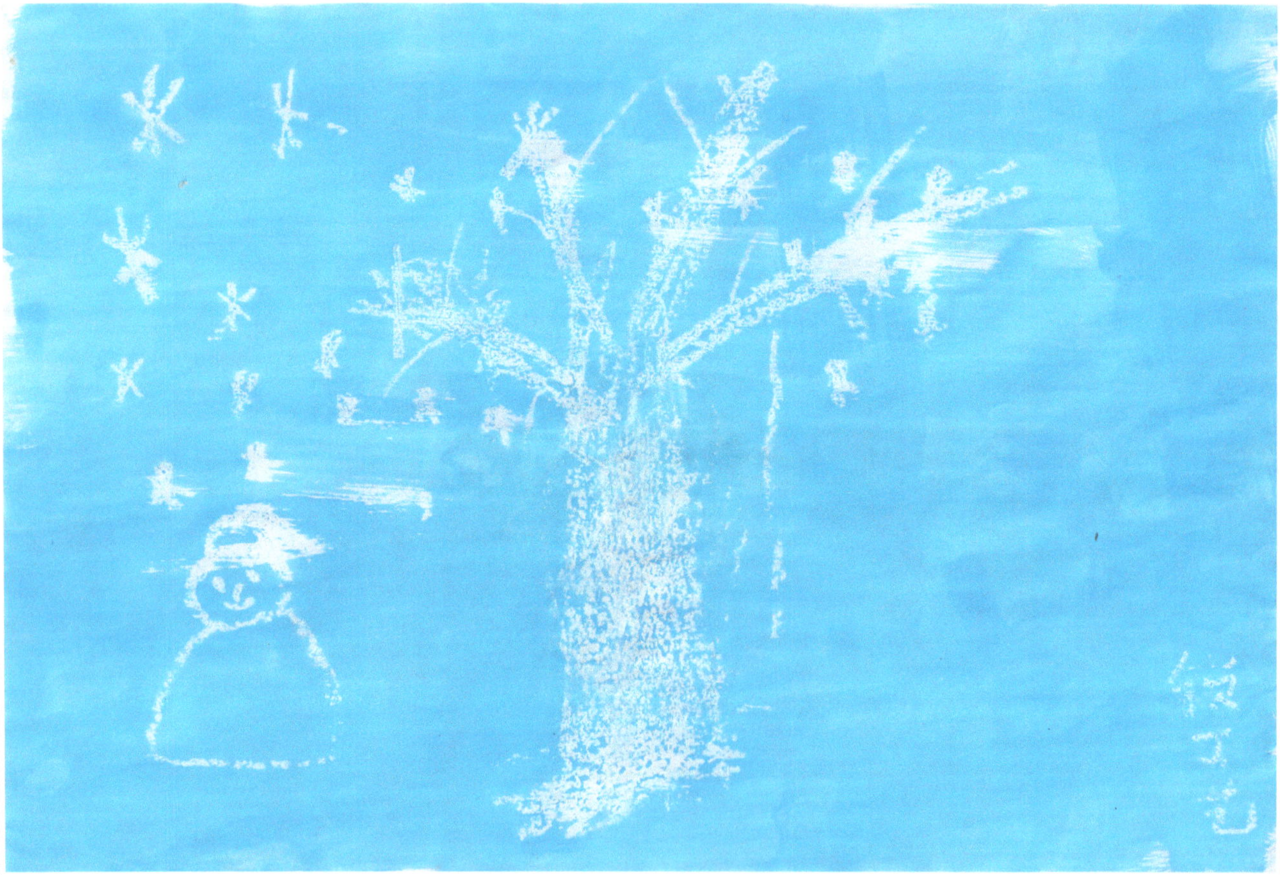

雪人和圣诞树（A snowman and a Christmas tree）

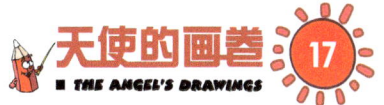

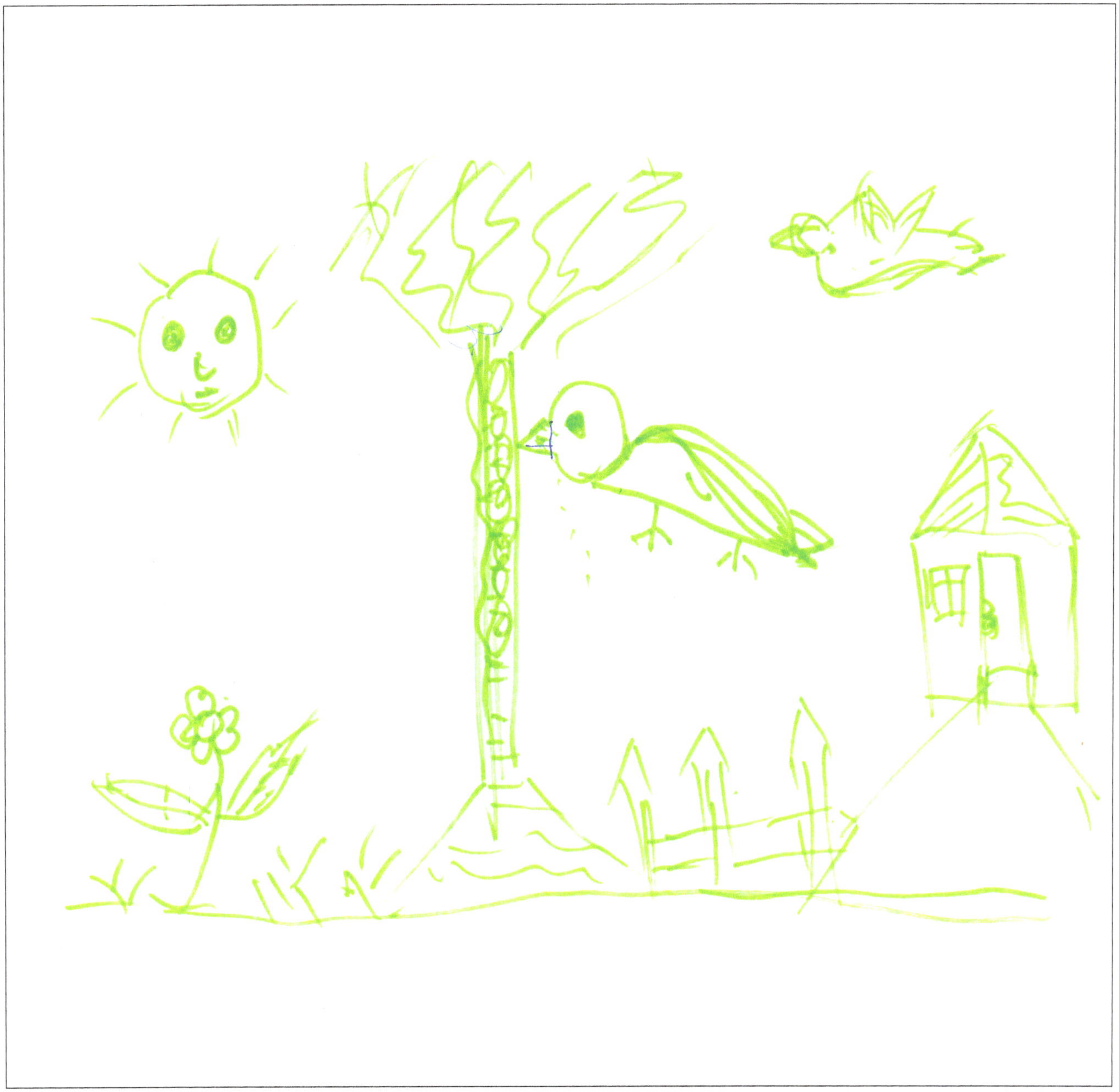

啄木鸟（Woodpeckers）

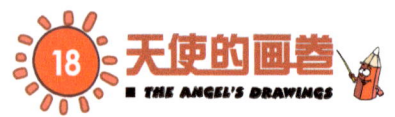

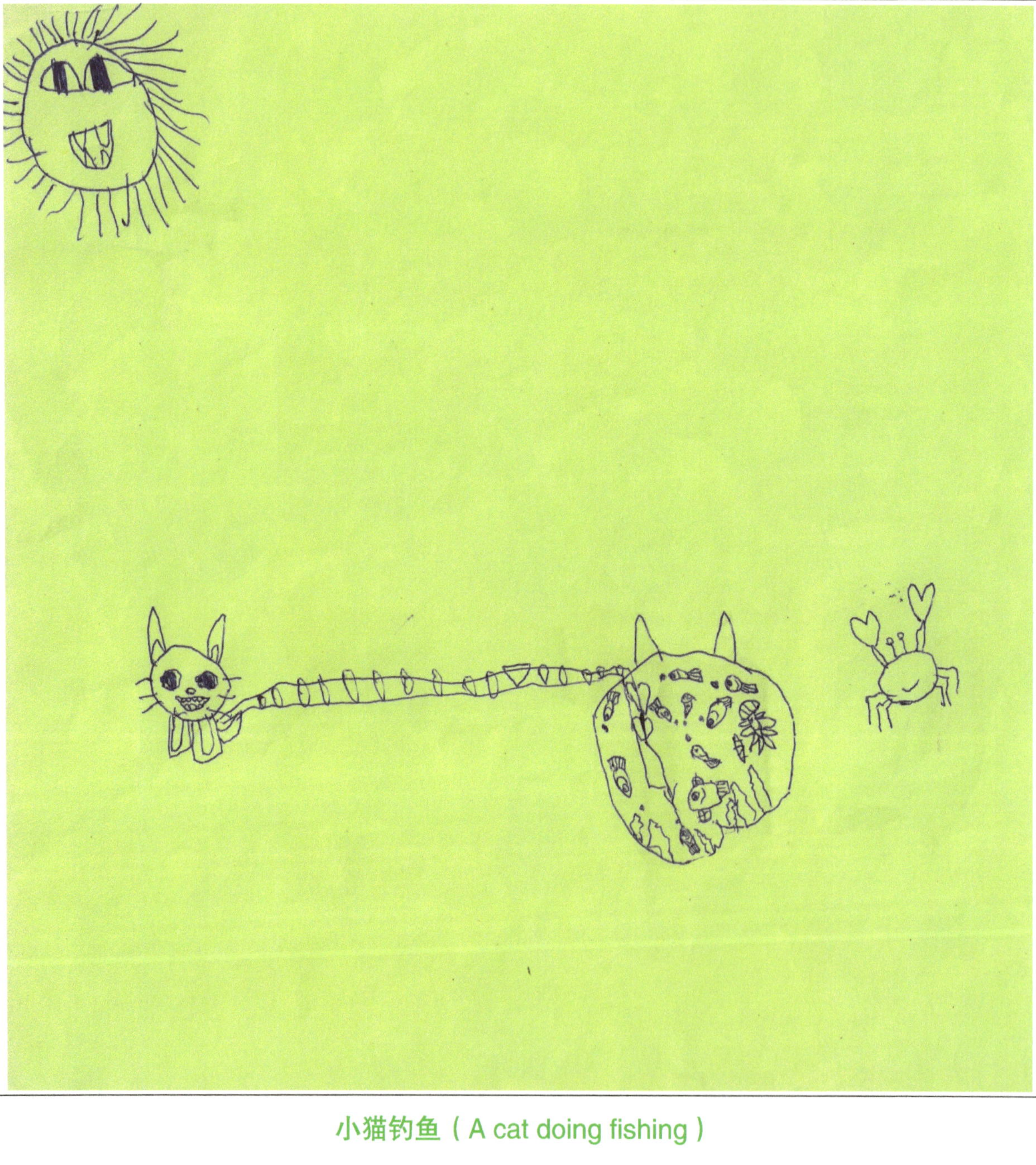

小猫钓鱼（A cat doing fishing）

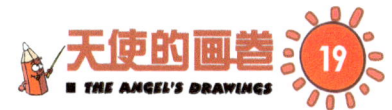

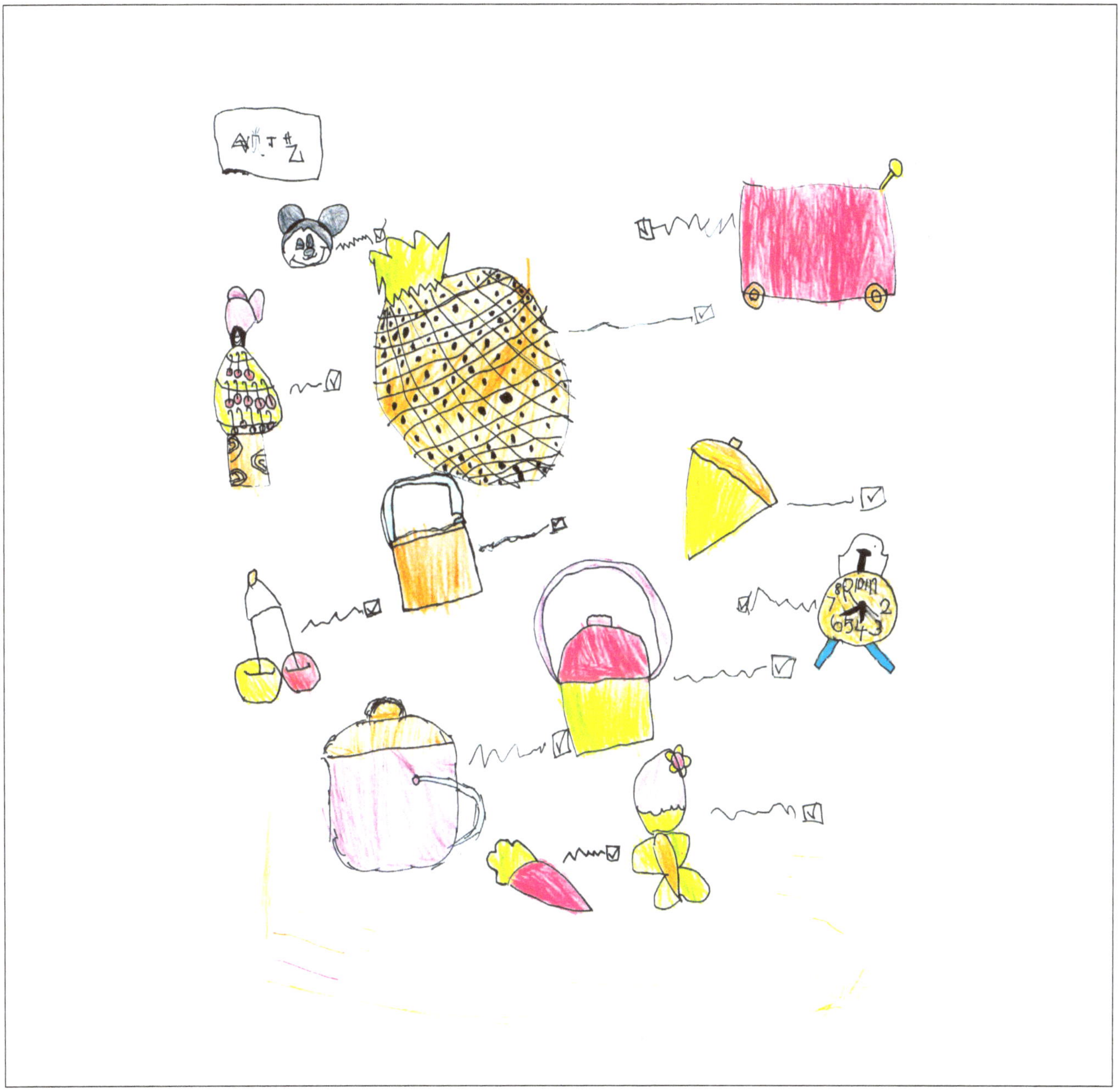

米奇的厨房（Mickey's kitchen）

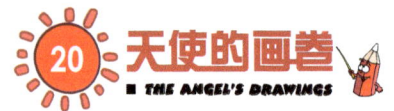
爸爸妈妈
姑姑 奶奶
好爱你们喔！
7.2月

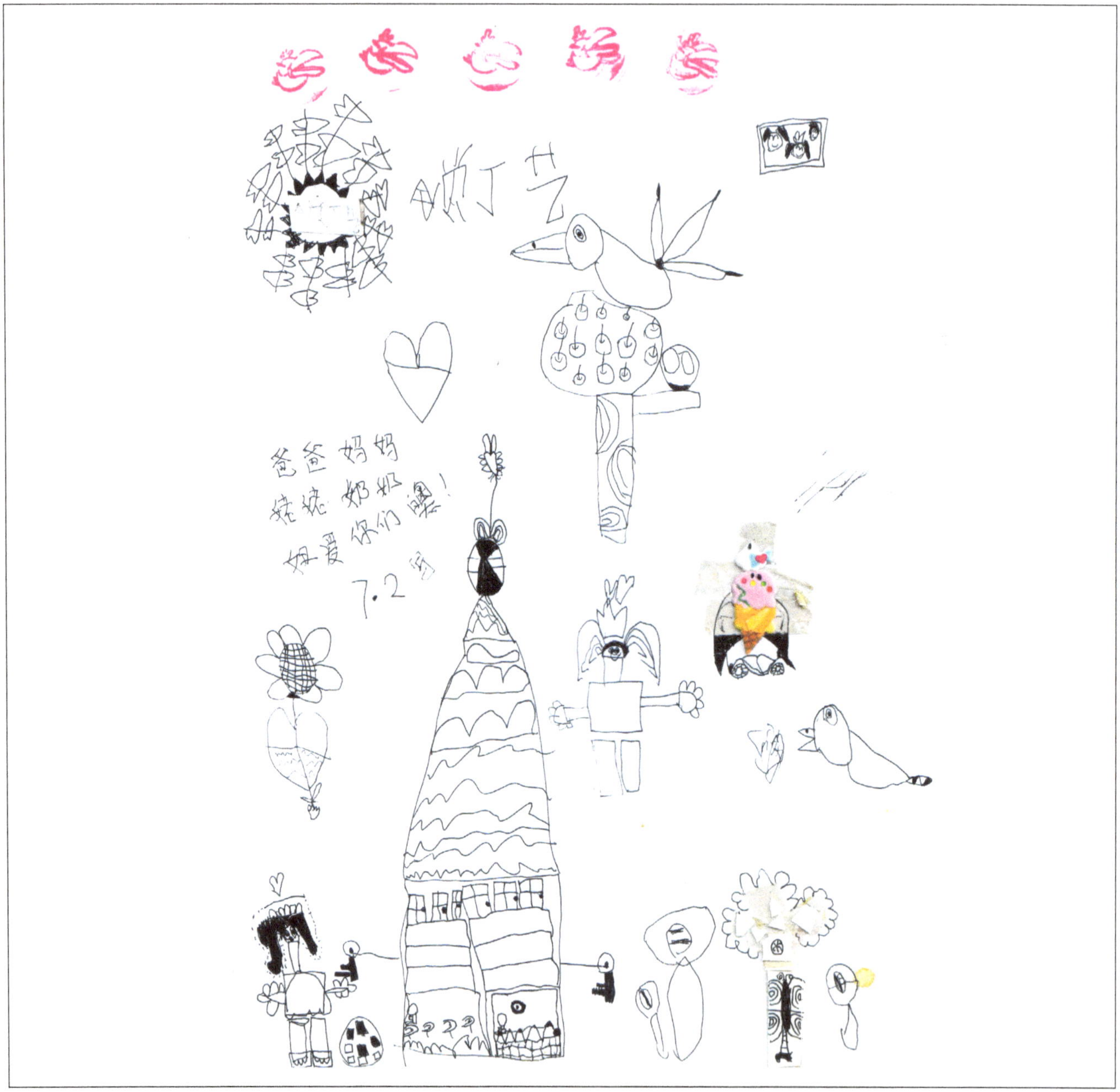

快乐的生活（A happy life）

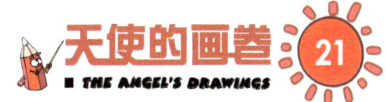

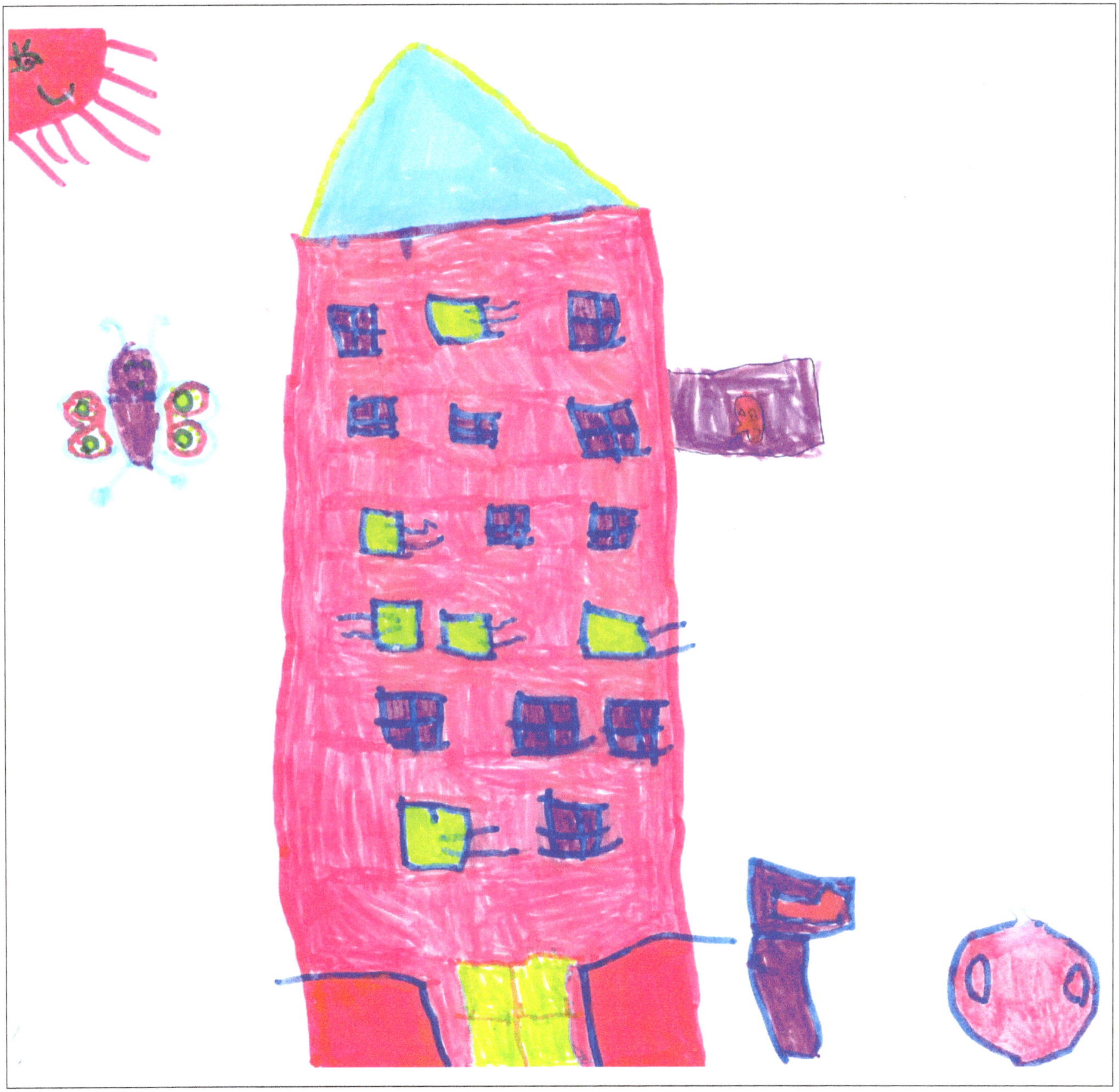

美丽的房子（A beautiful house）

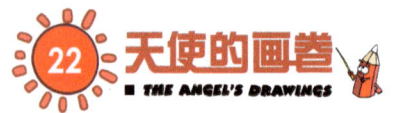

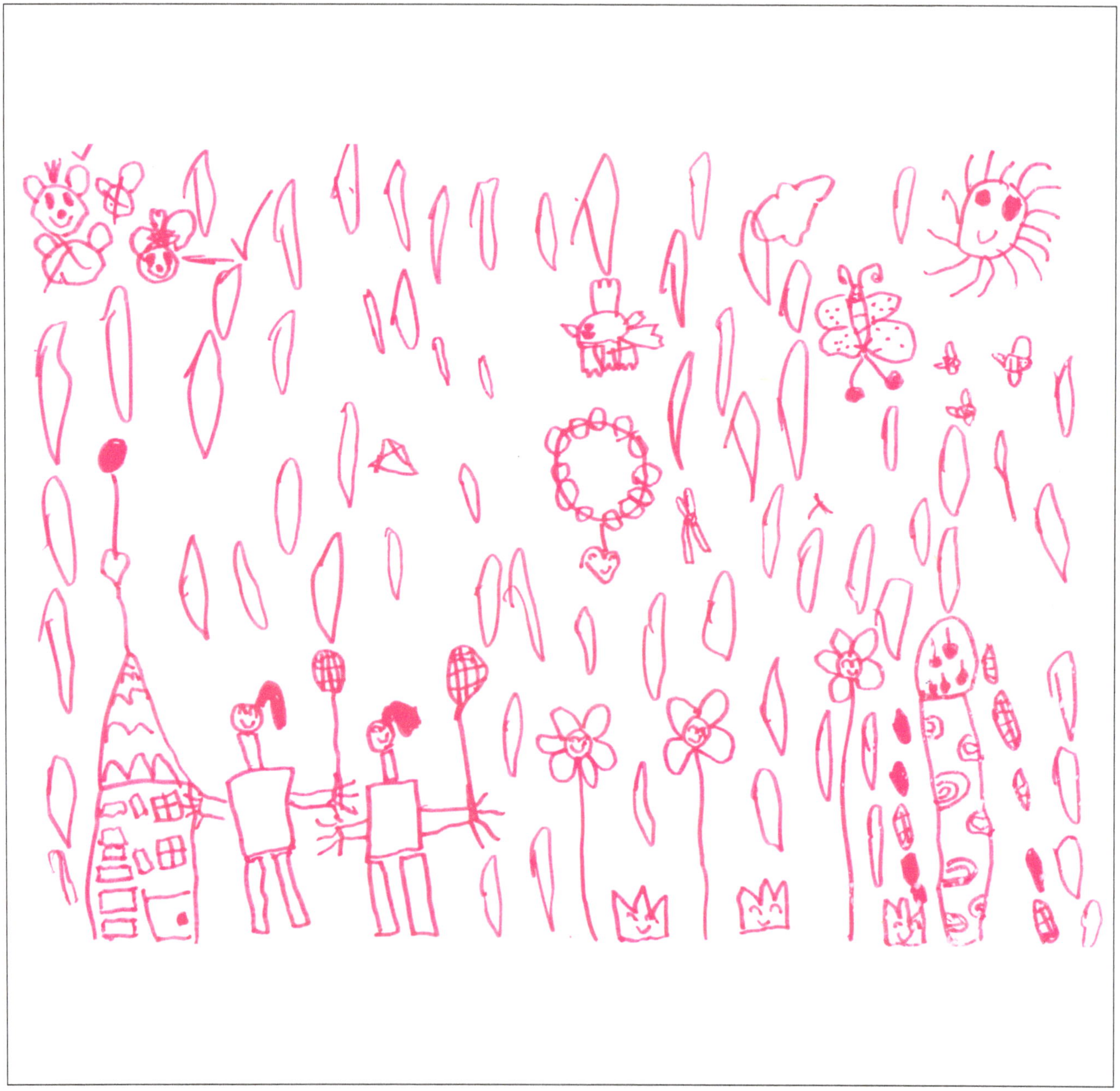

下雨了（Raining）

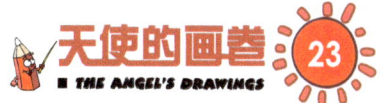

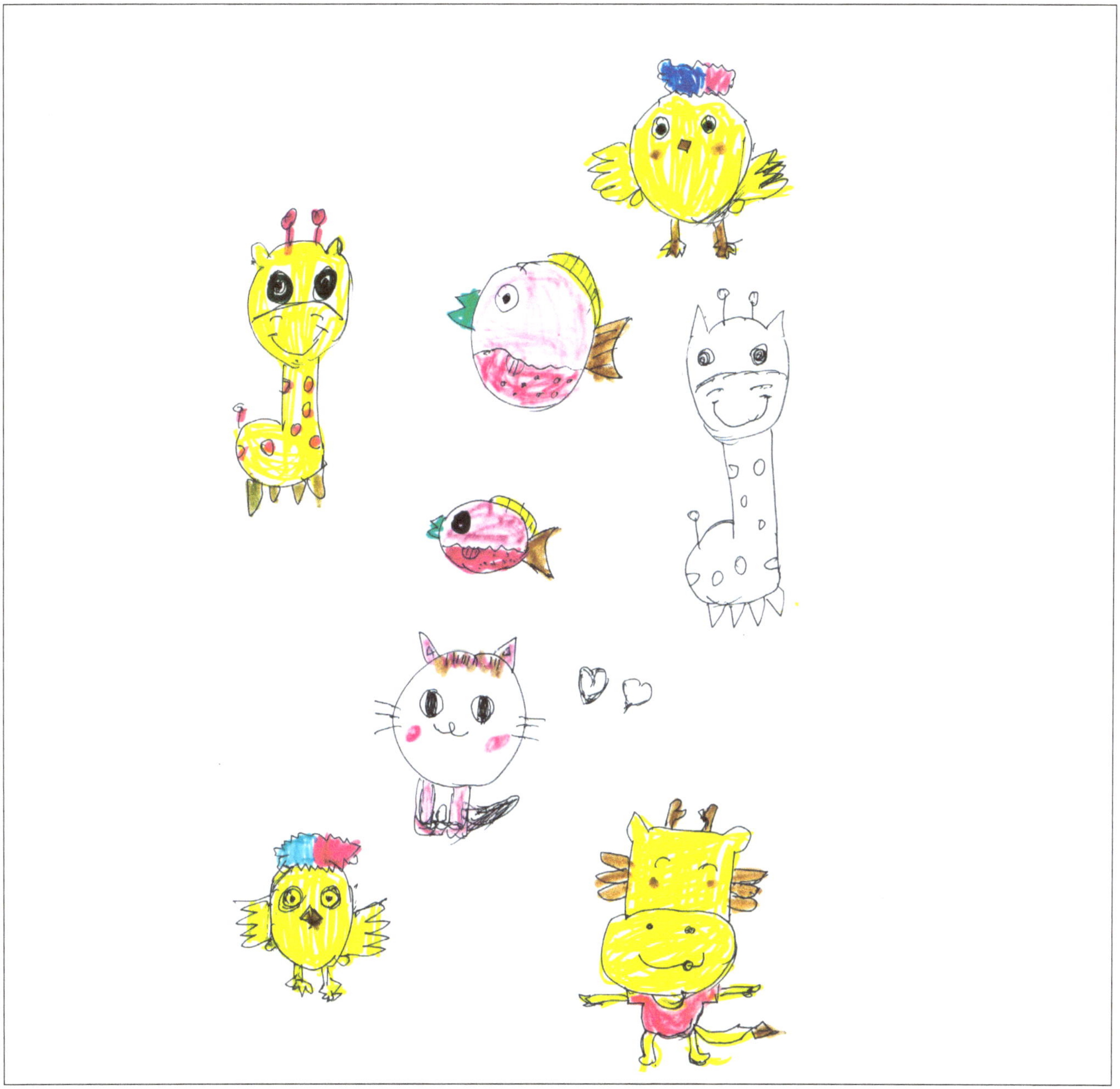

开心的小动物（Happy little animals）

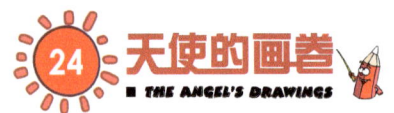

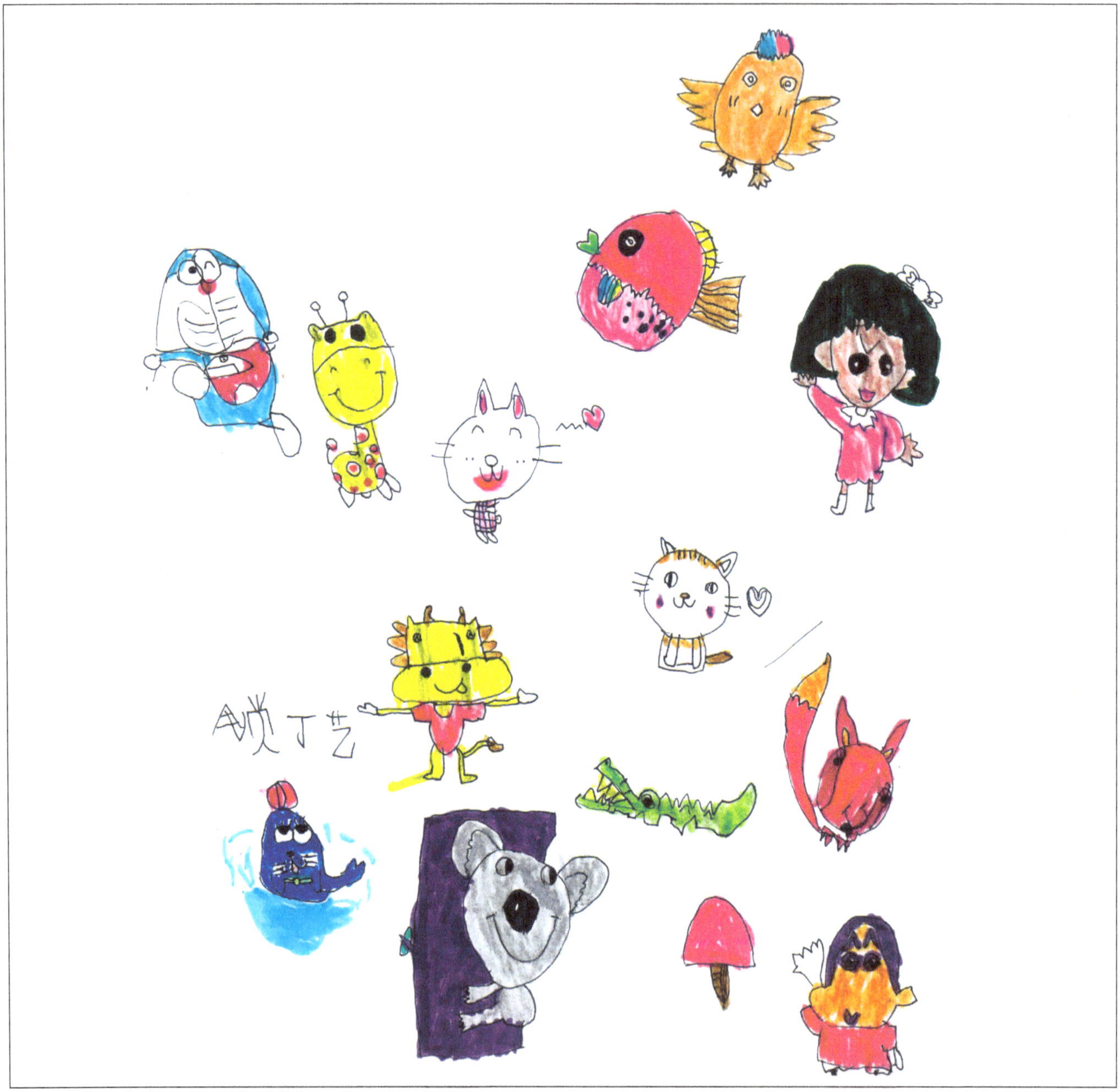

快乐的派对（A great party）

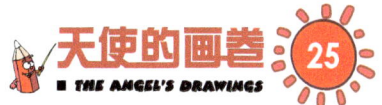

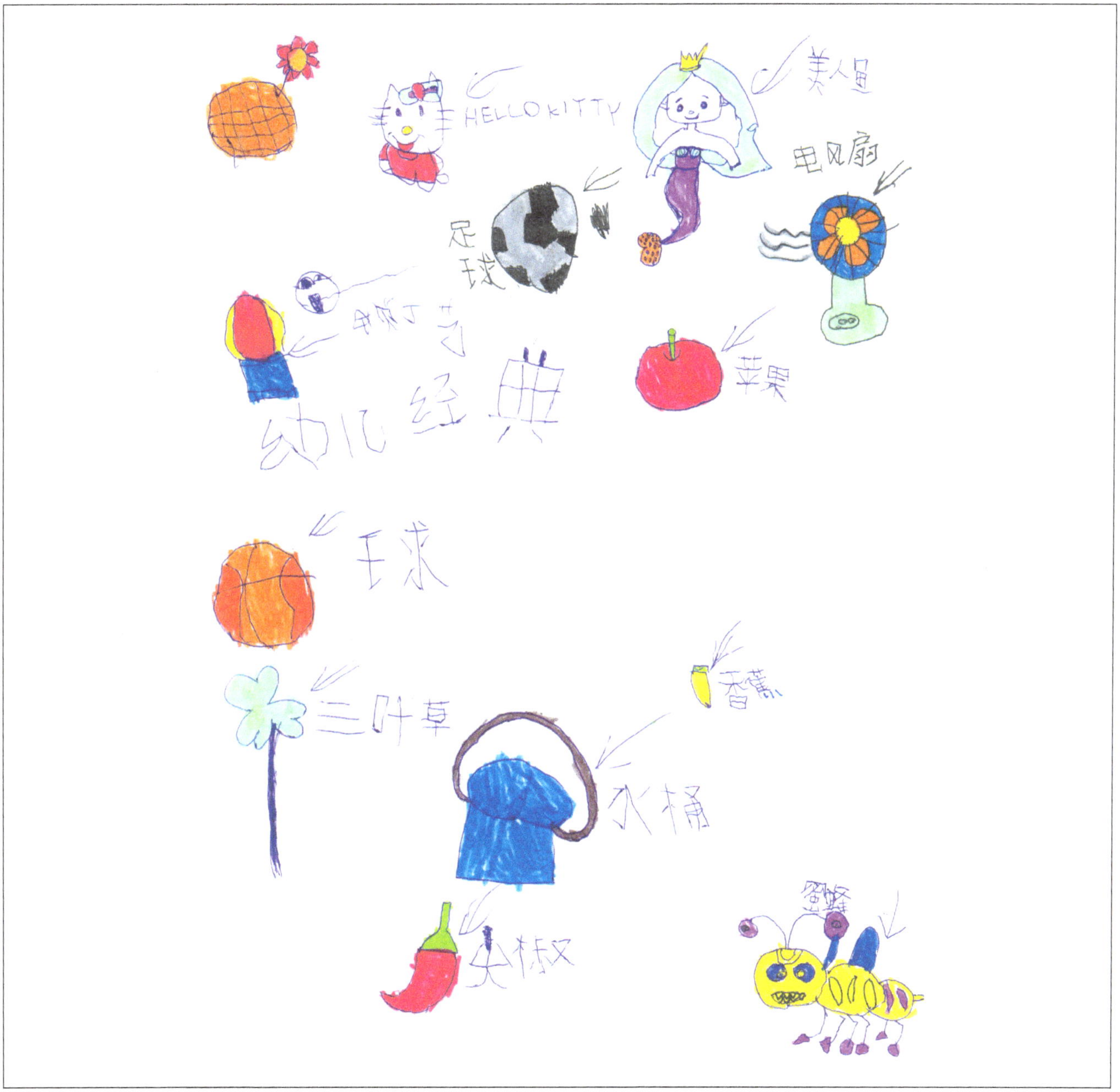

HELLO KITTY

美人鱼

电风扇

足球

啊叮当

幼儿经典

苹果

玉球

三叶草

香蕉

水桶

尖椒

我喜爱的东西（My favorite things）

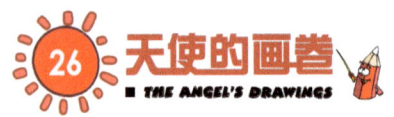

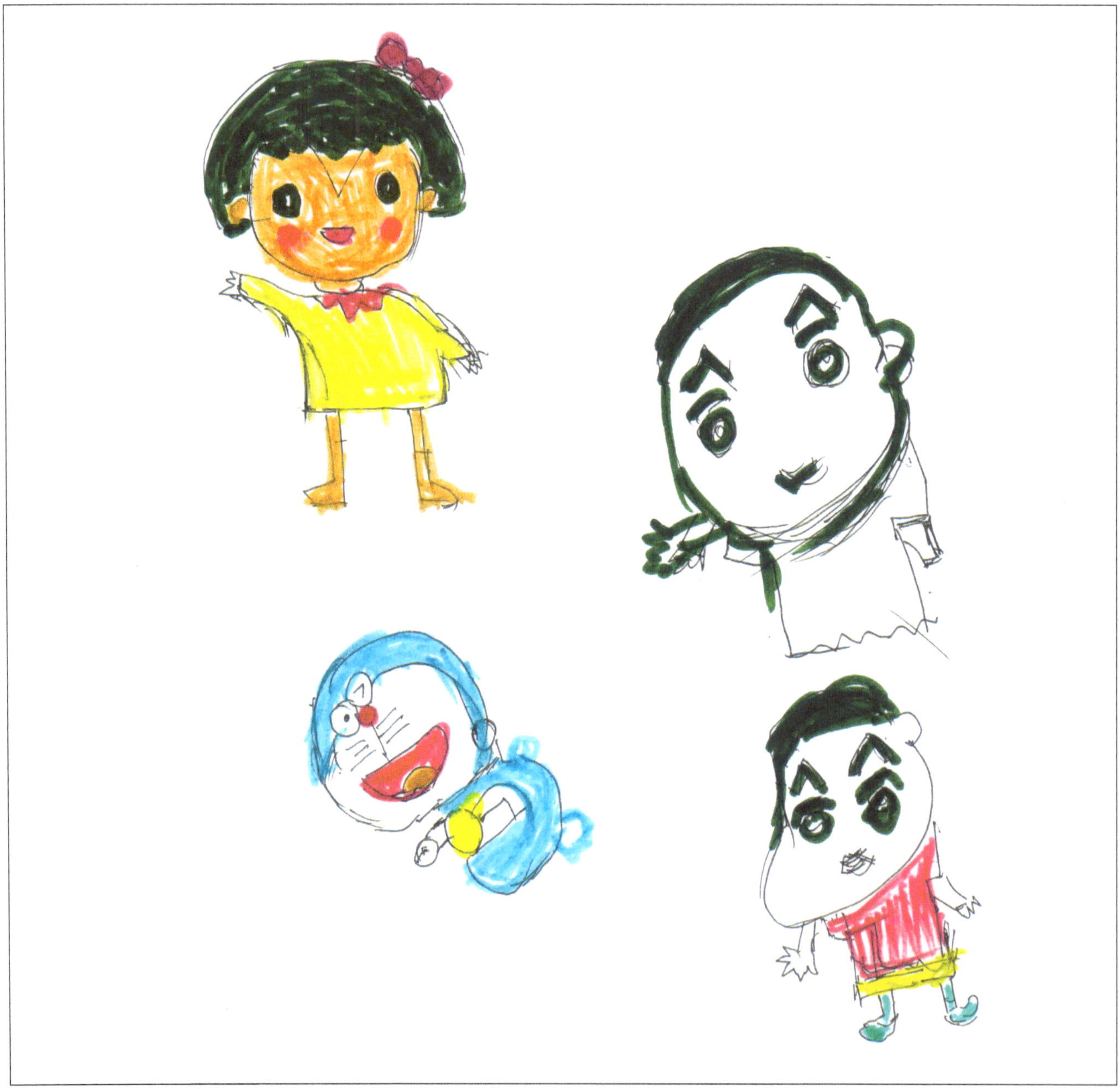

姥姥和我画的画儿（My grandma and my partings）

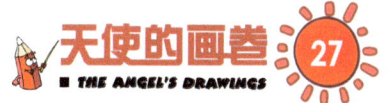

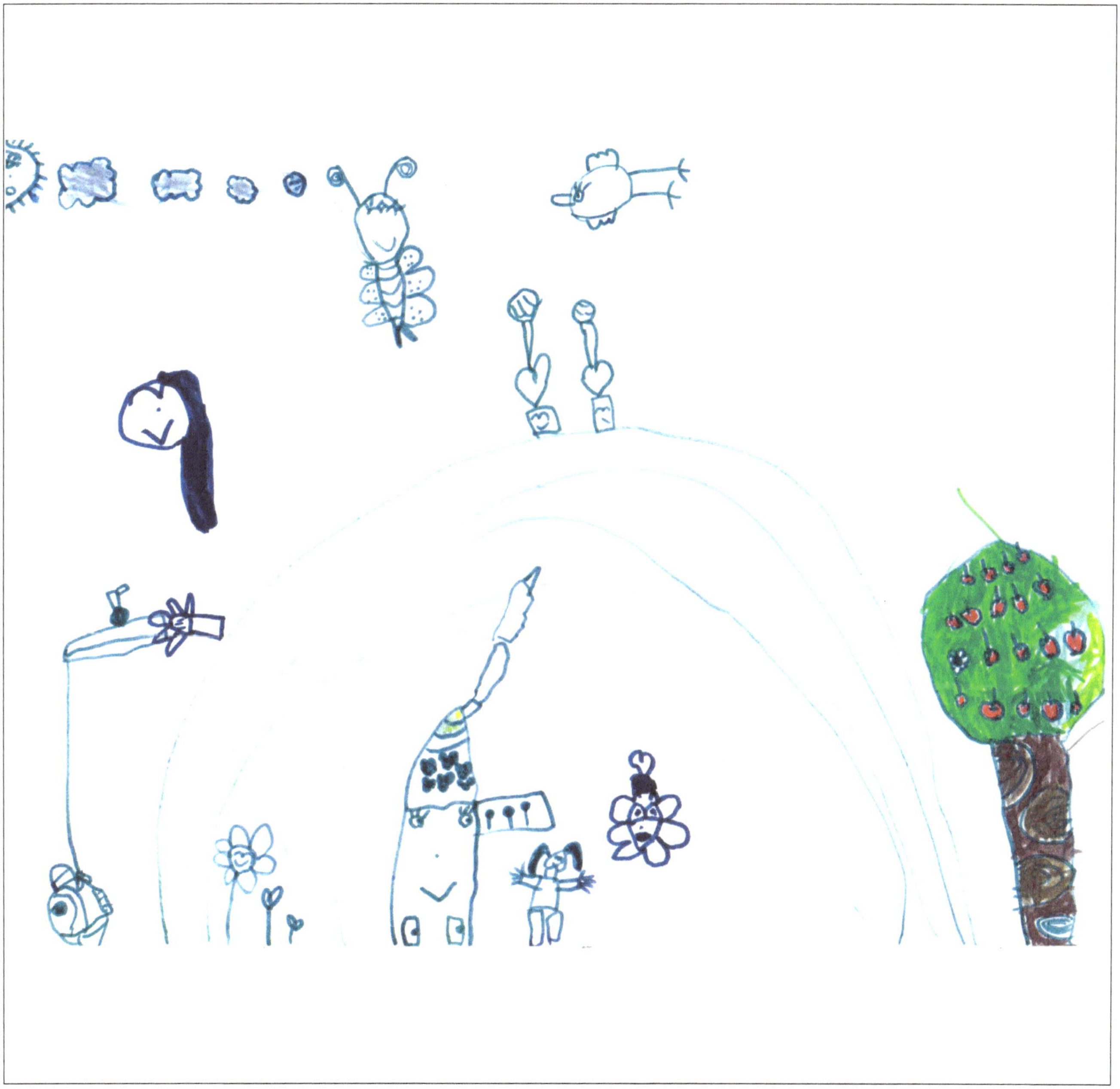

彩虹世界 (A world of rainbow)

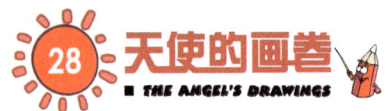

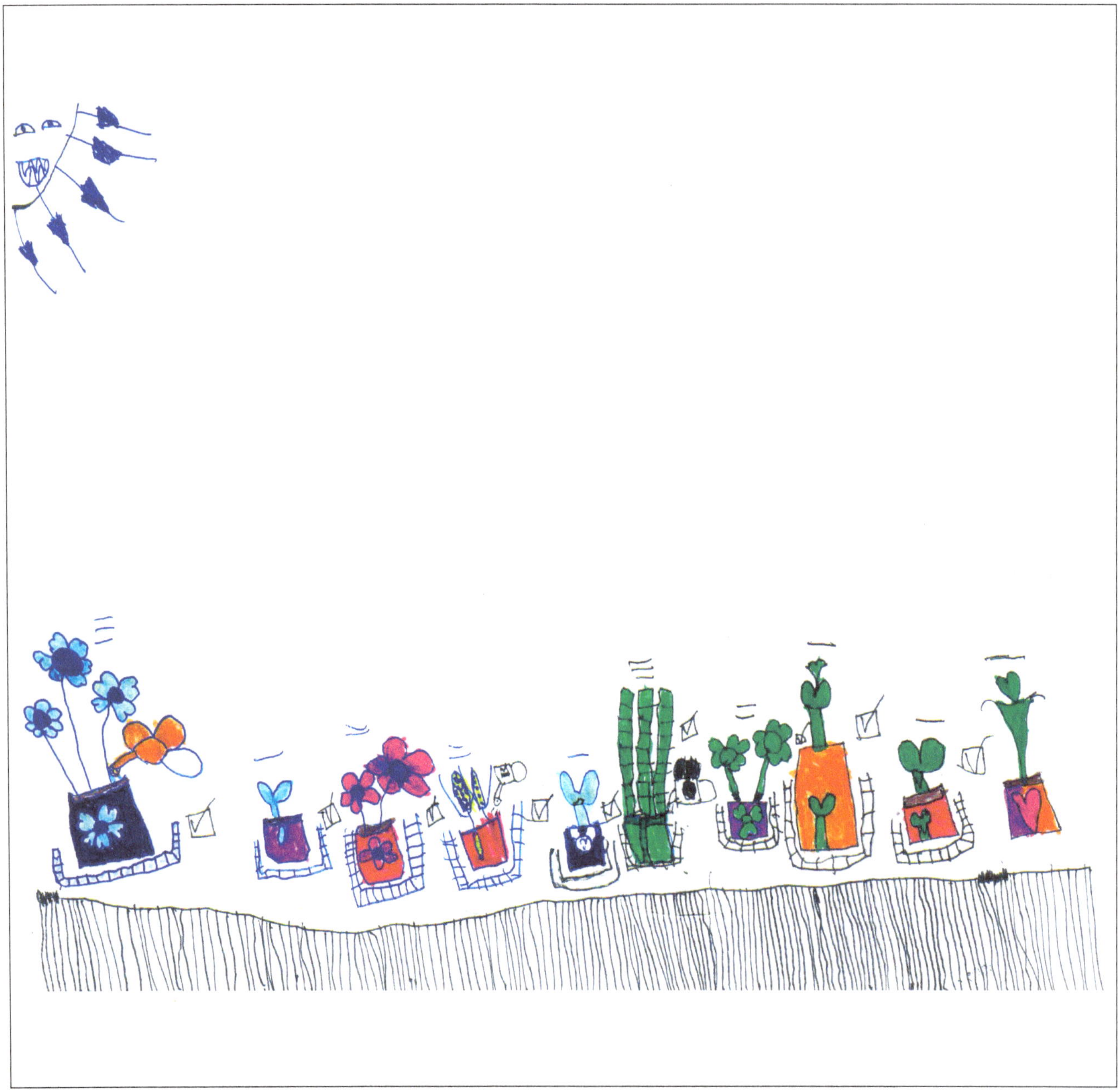

阳台上的花园（A garden on the balcony）

第二部分 色彩

Chapter Two: Colors

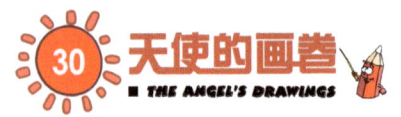
猫头鹰（An owl）

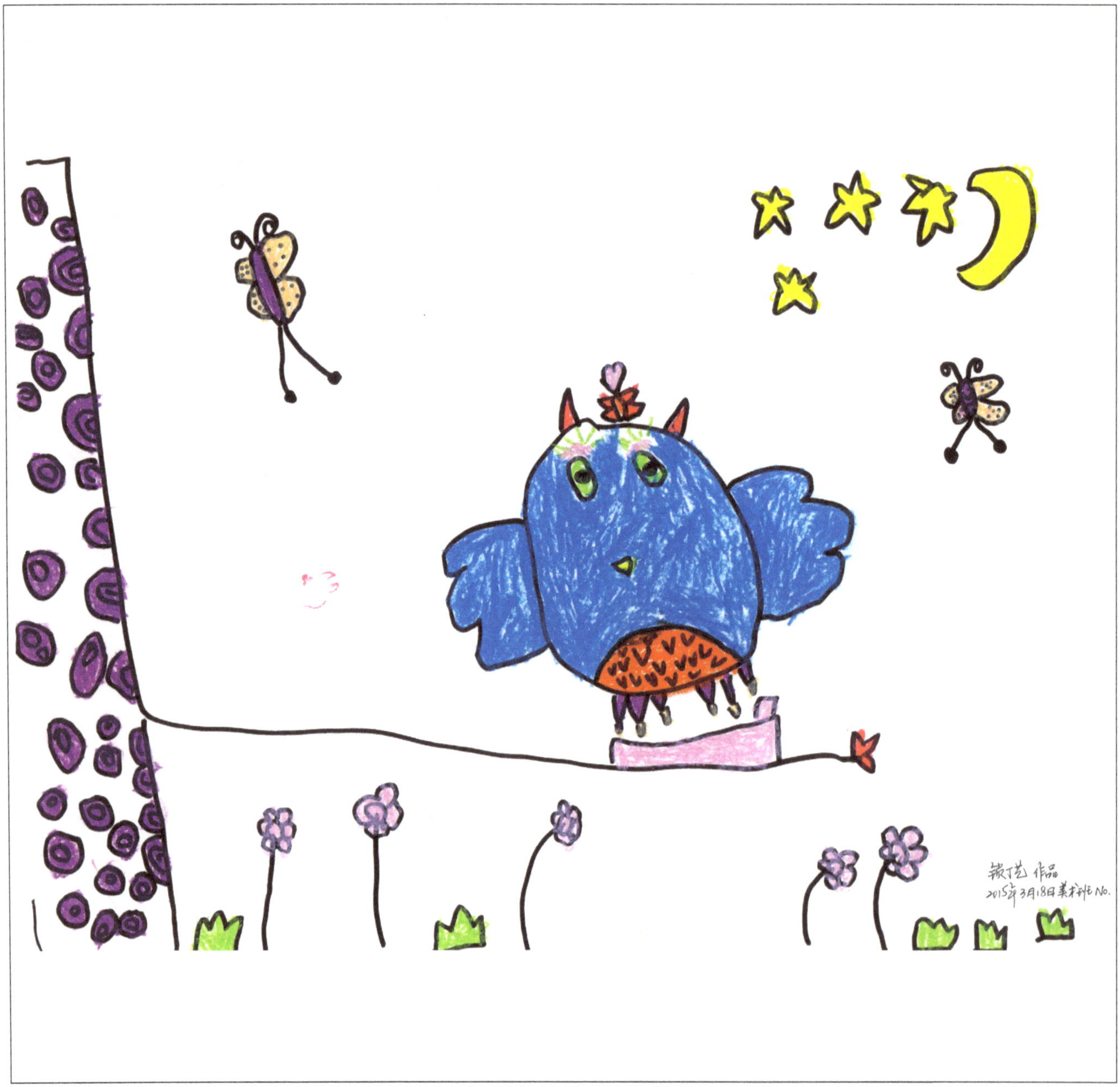

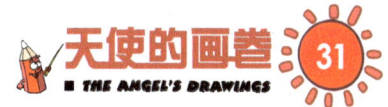

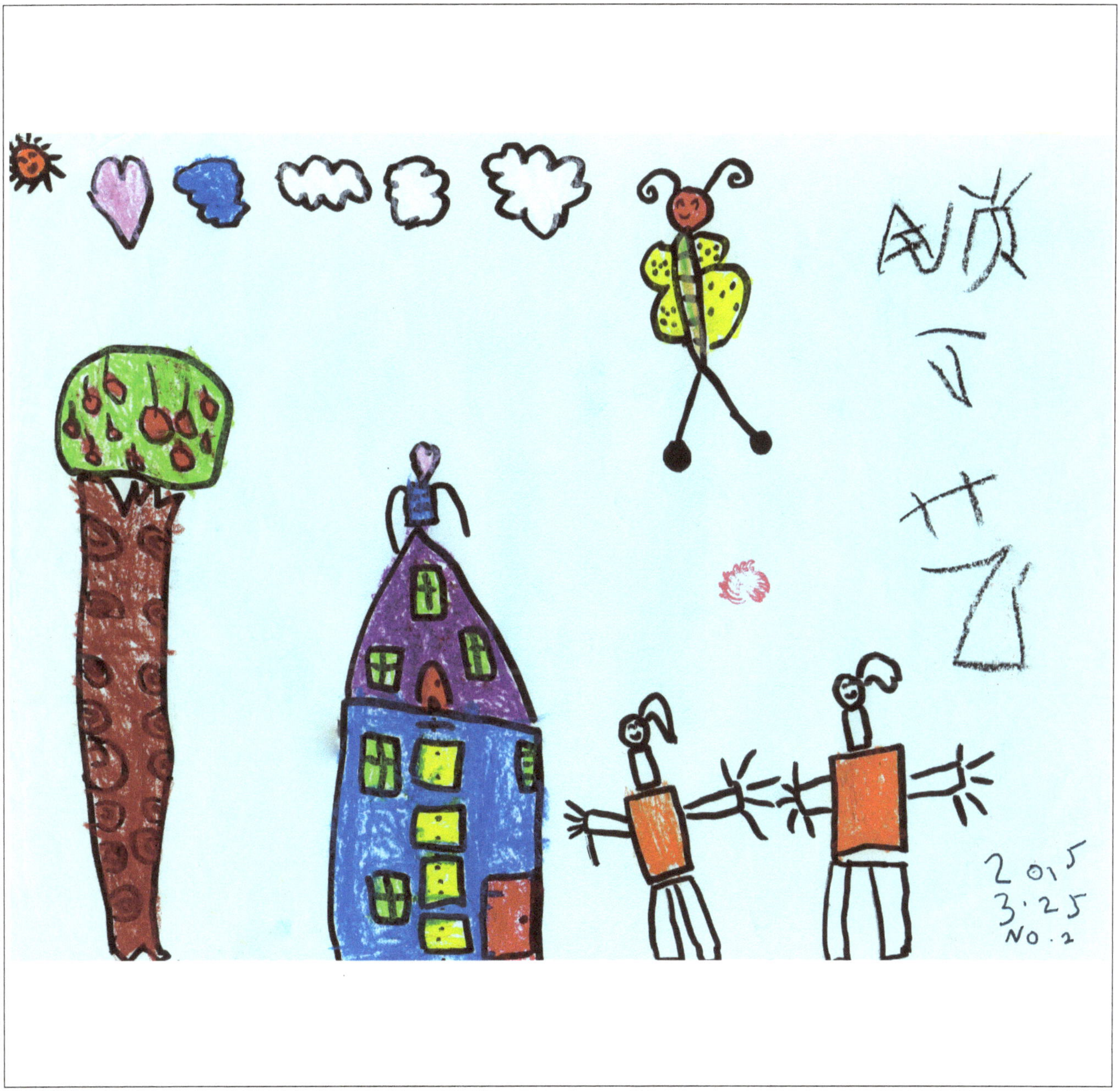

米奇和妈妈的家（Mickey, his mom and his home）

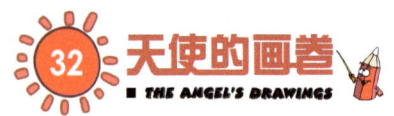

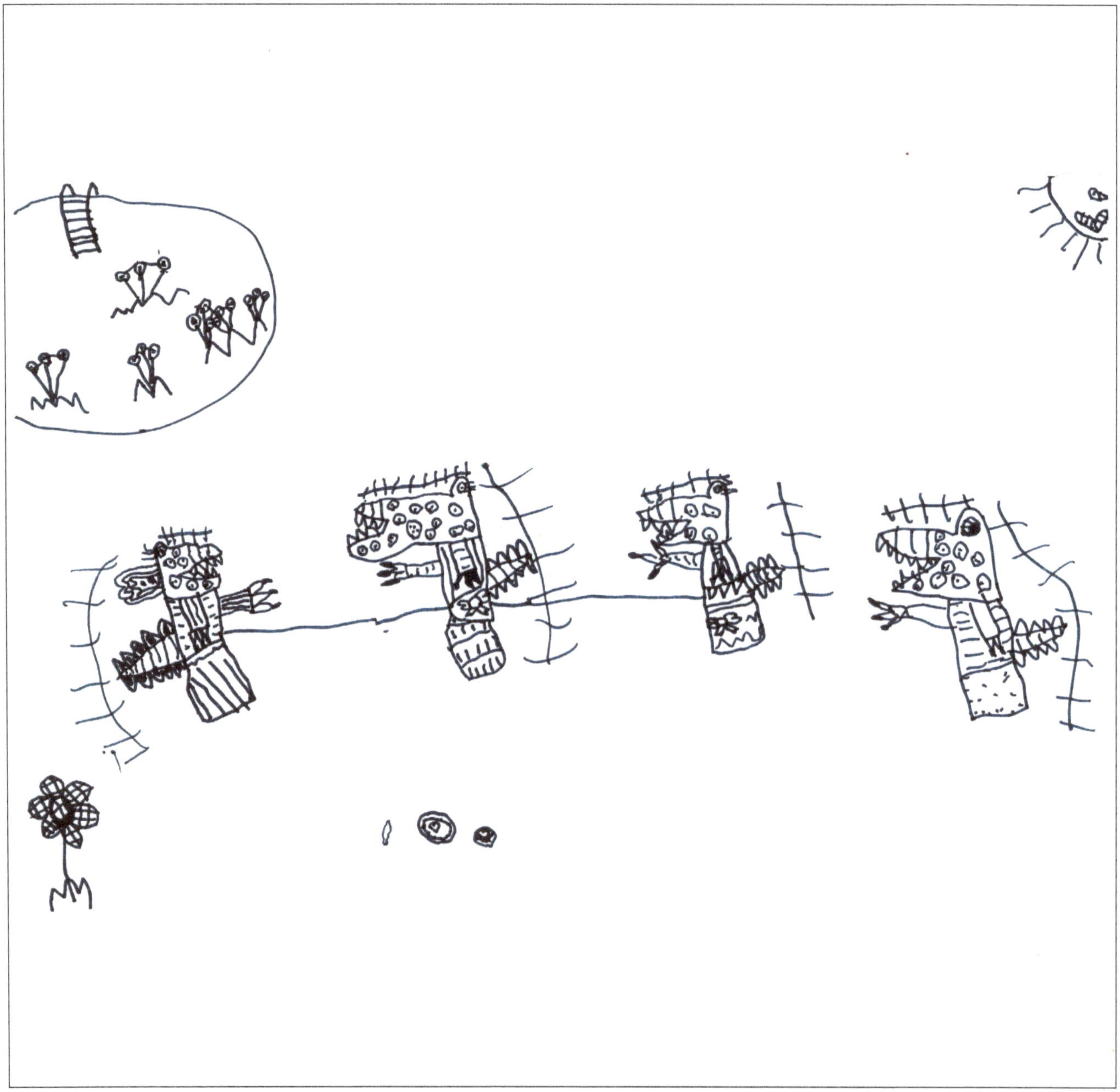

鳄鱼家族（Crocodiles' family）

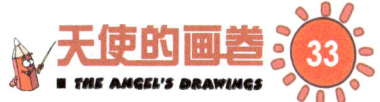

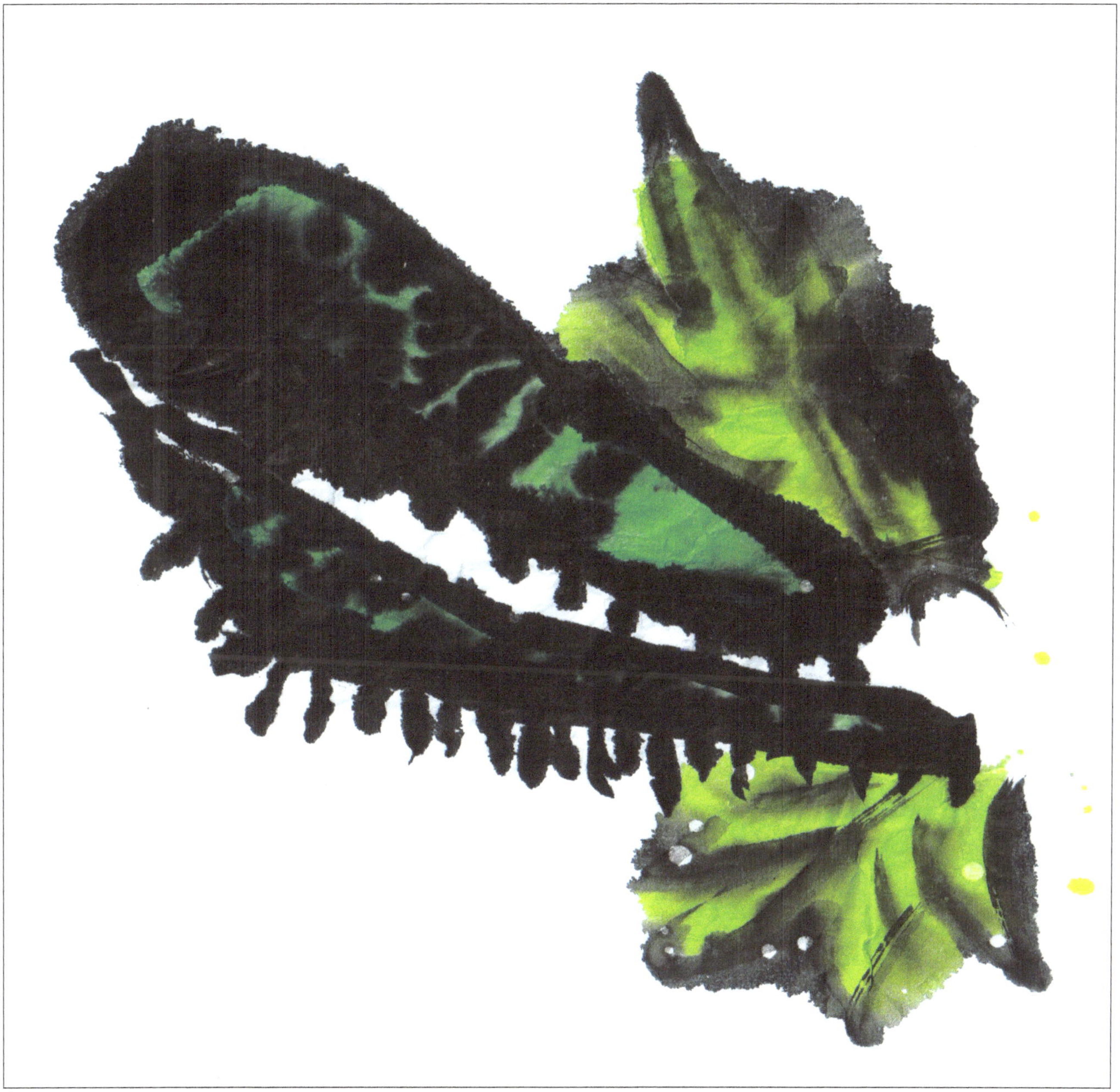

黄瓜（Cucumbers）

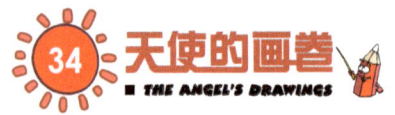

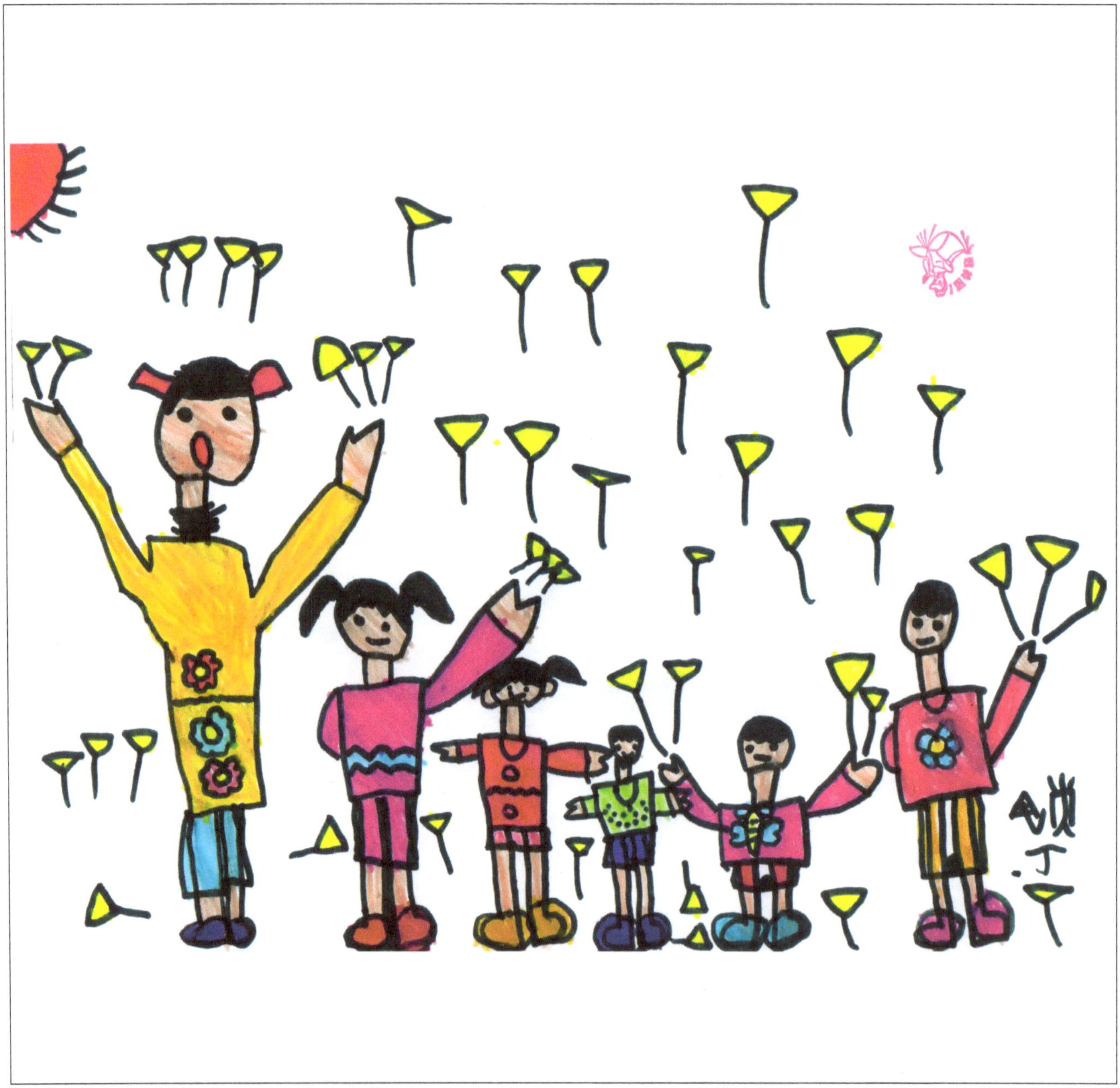

小朋友捡树叶（Children picking leaves）

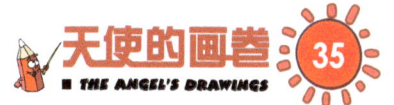

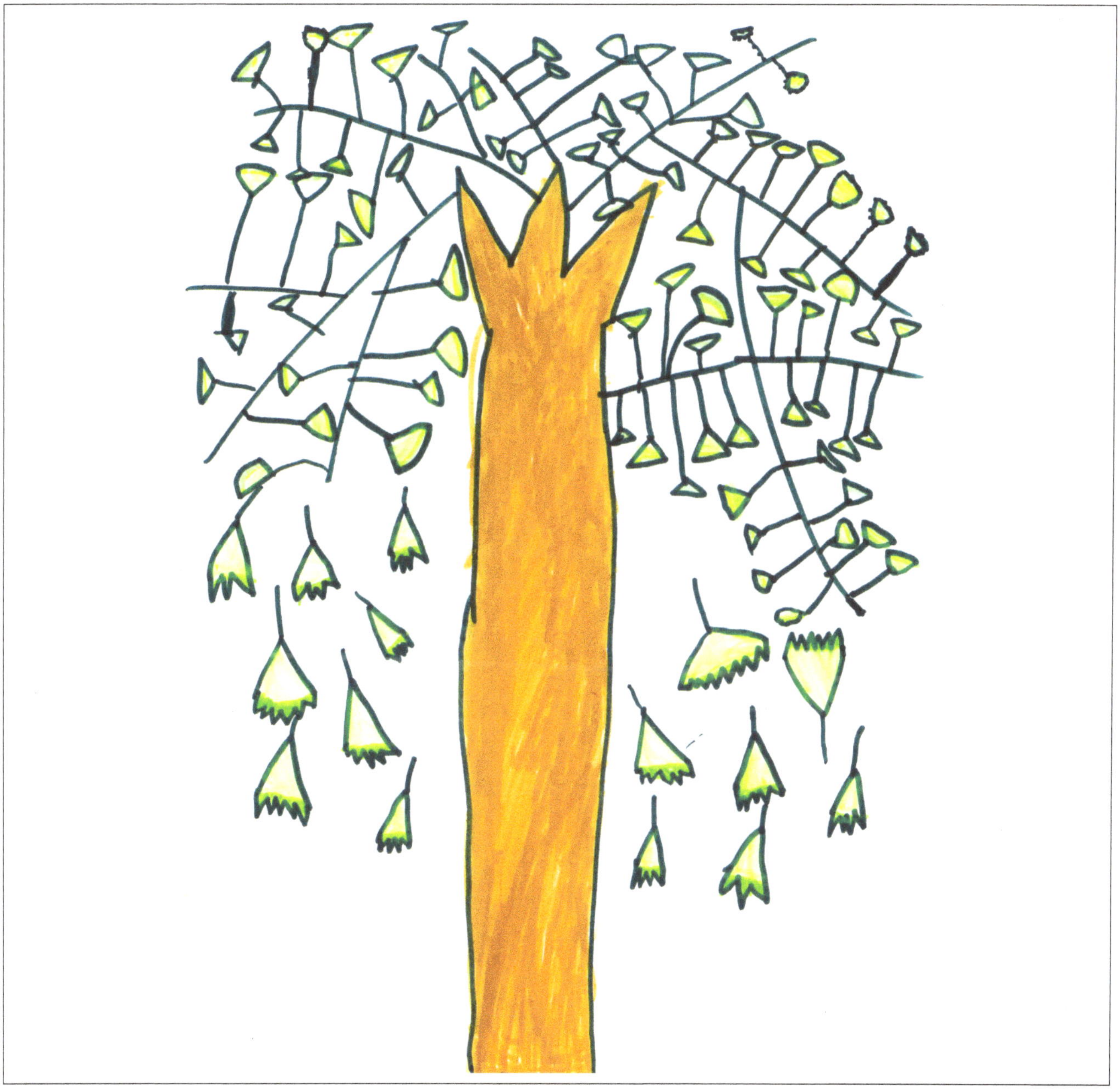

银杏树（A ginkgo tree）

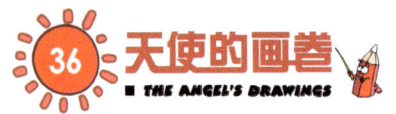

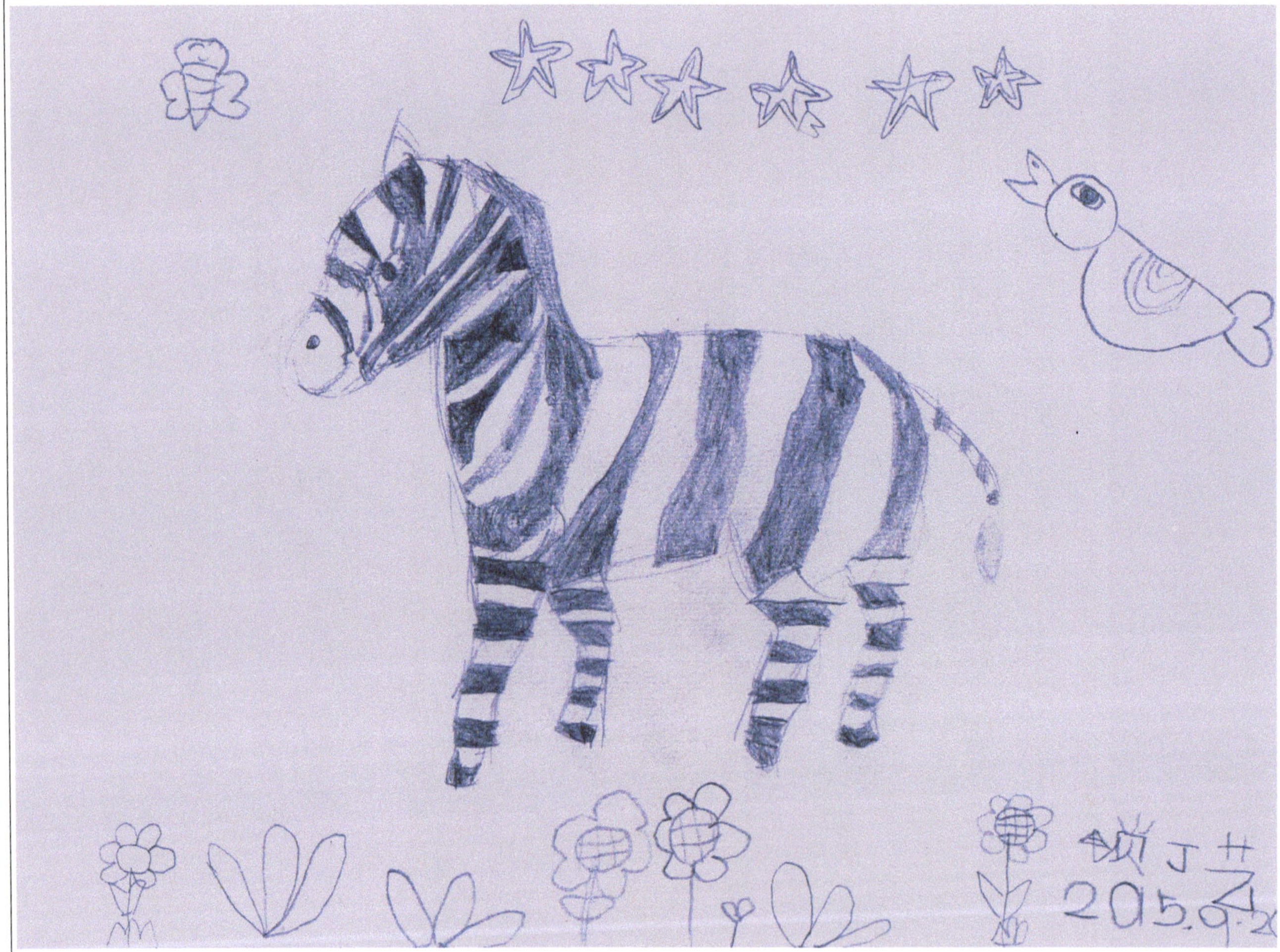

斑马（A zebra）

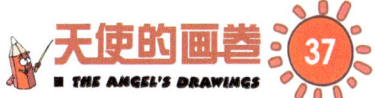

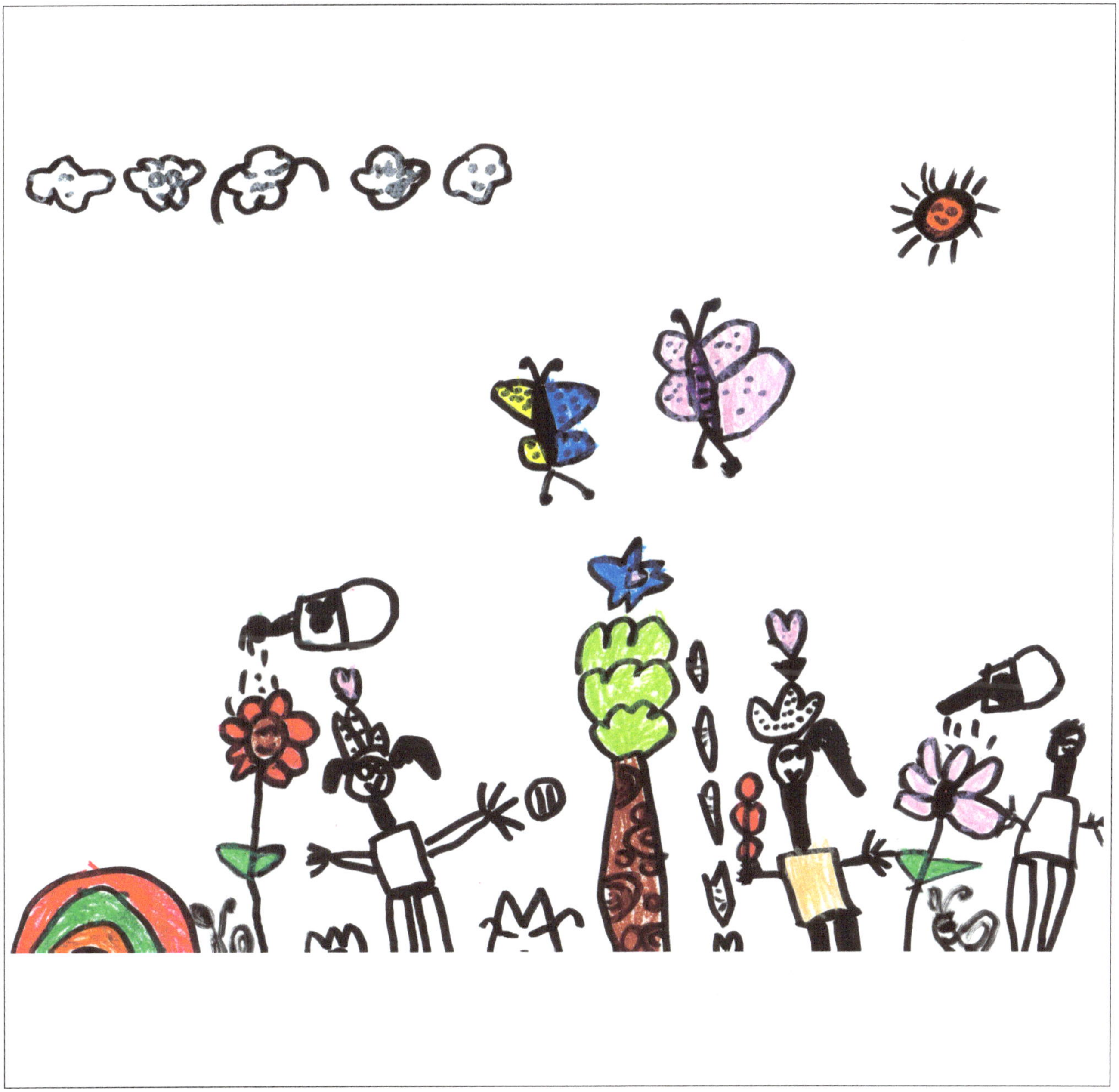

一家人浇花（A family watering flowers）

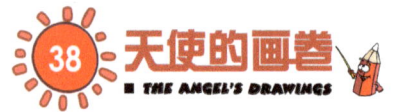

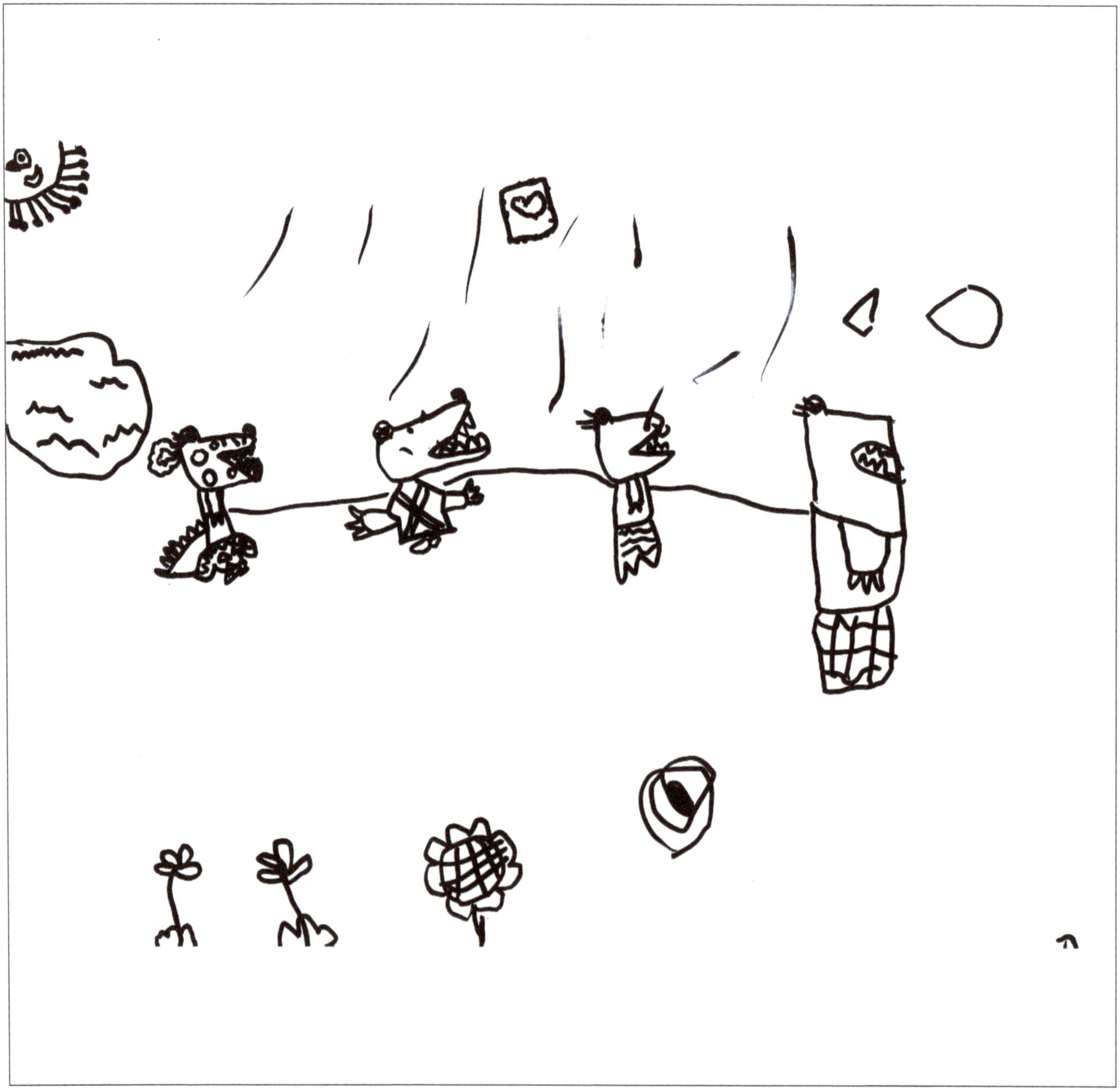

鳄鱼（Crocodiles）

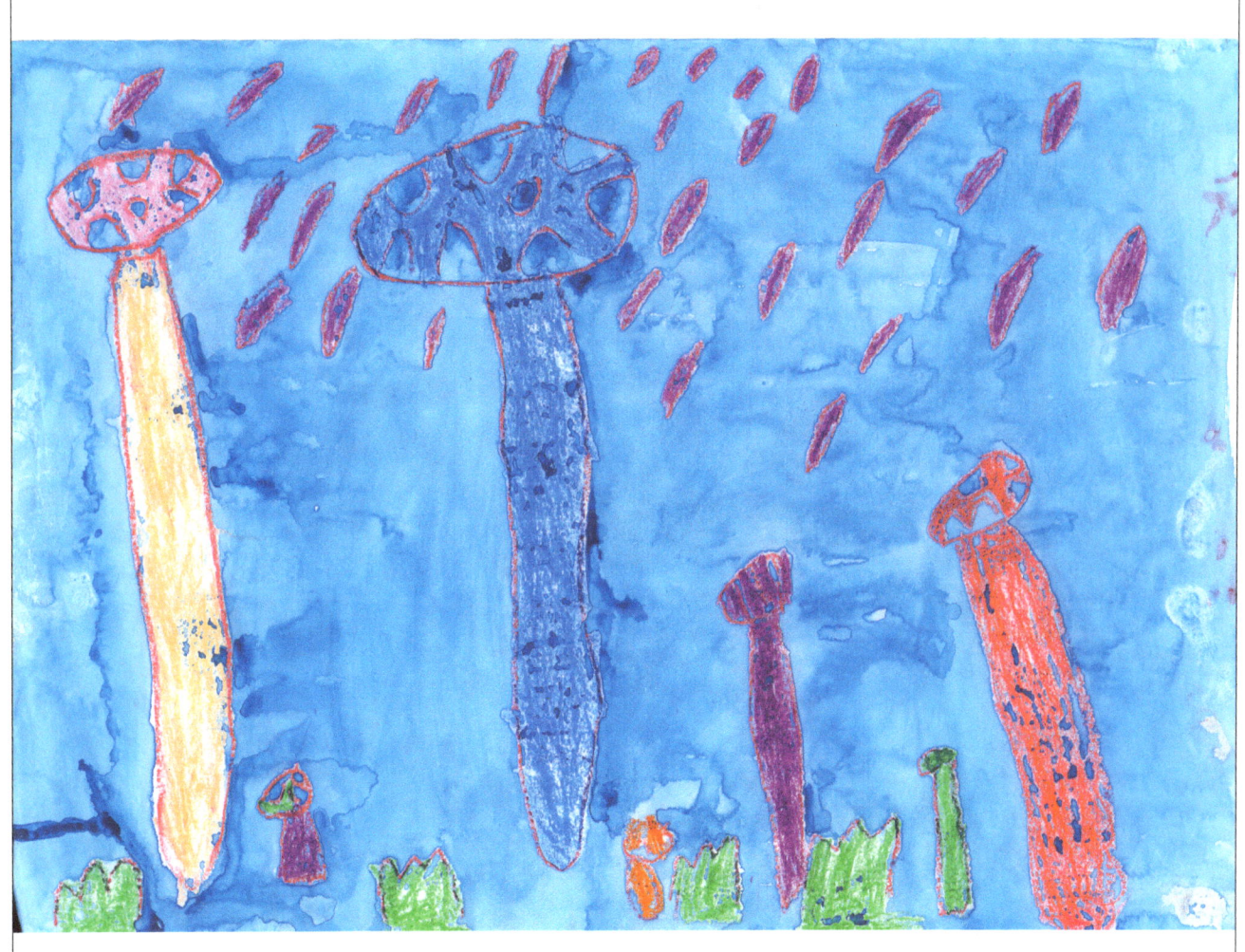

蘑菇（Mushrooms）

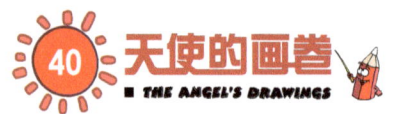
窗前的鲜花（Flowers on the window）

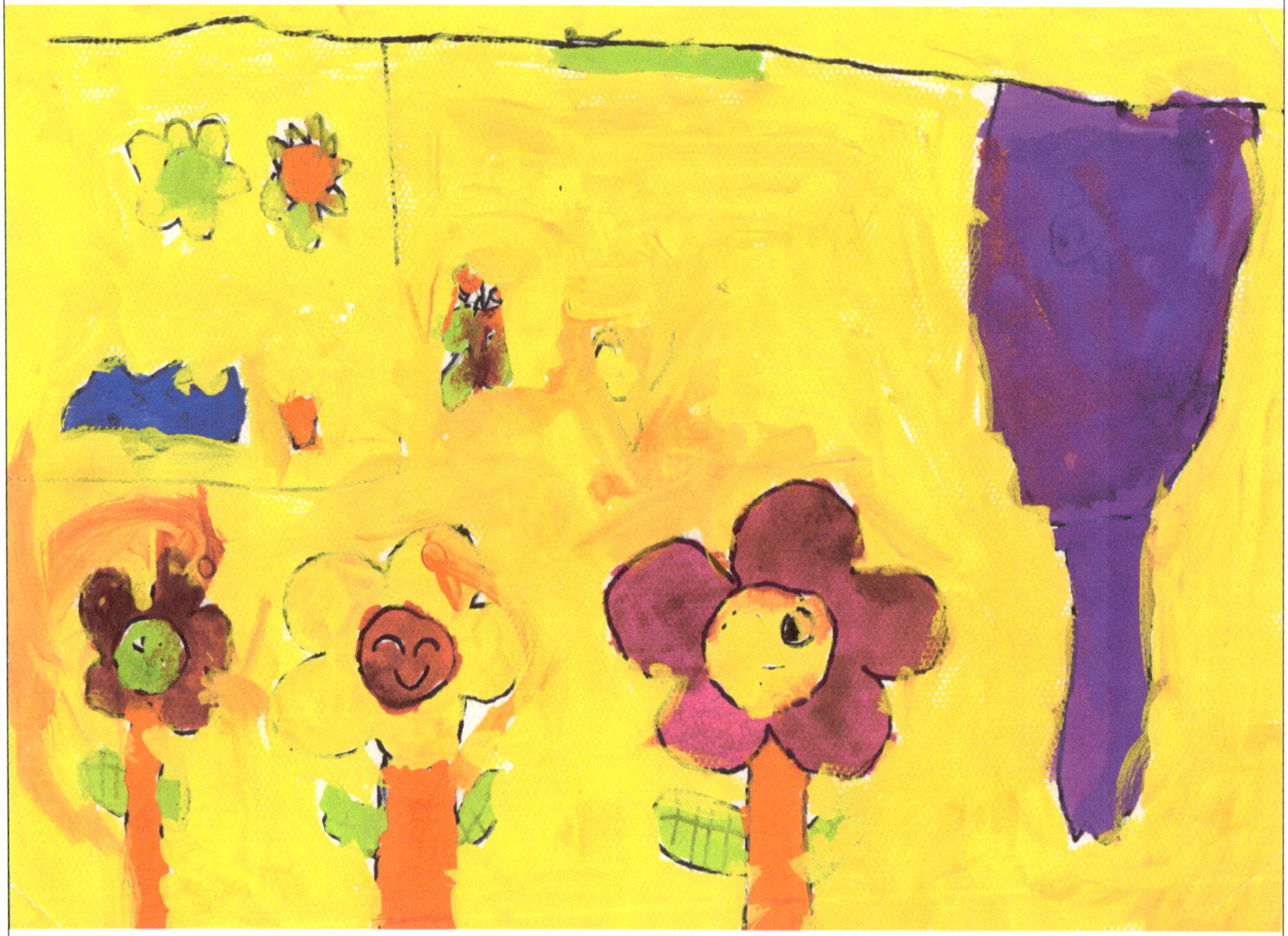

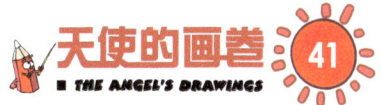

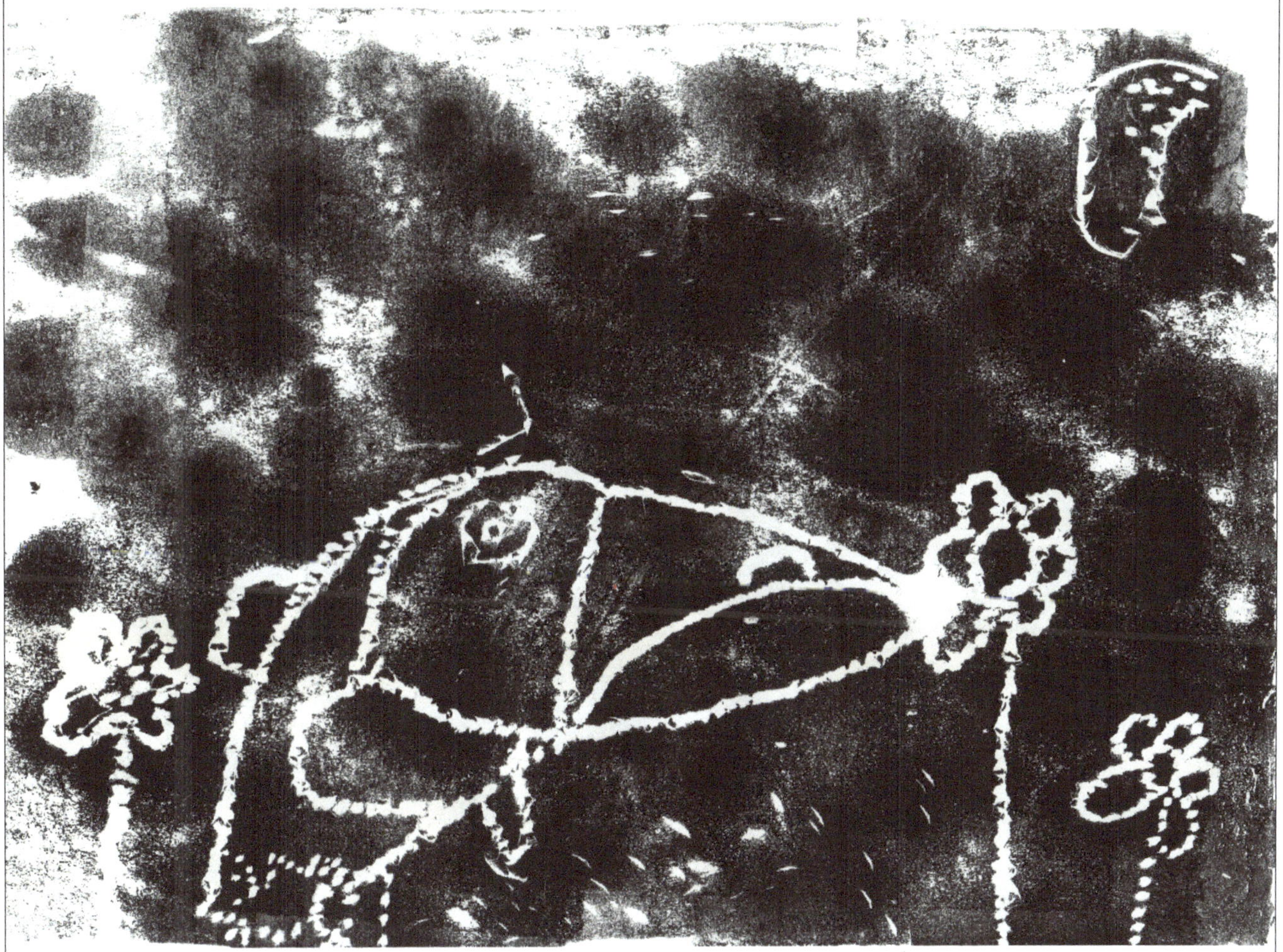

乌鸦（A crow）

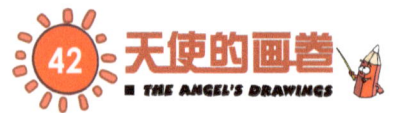

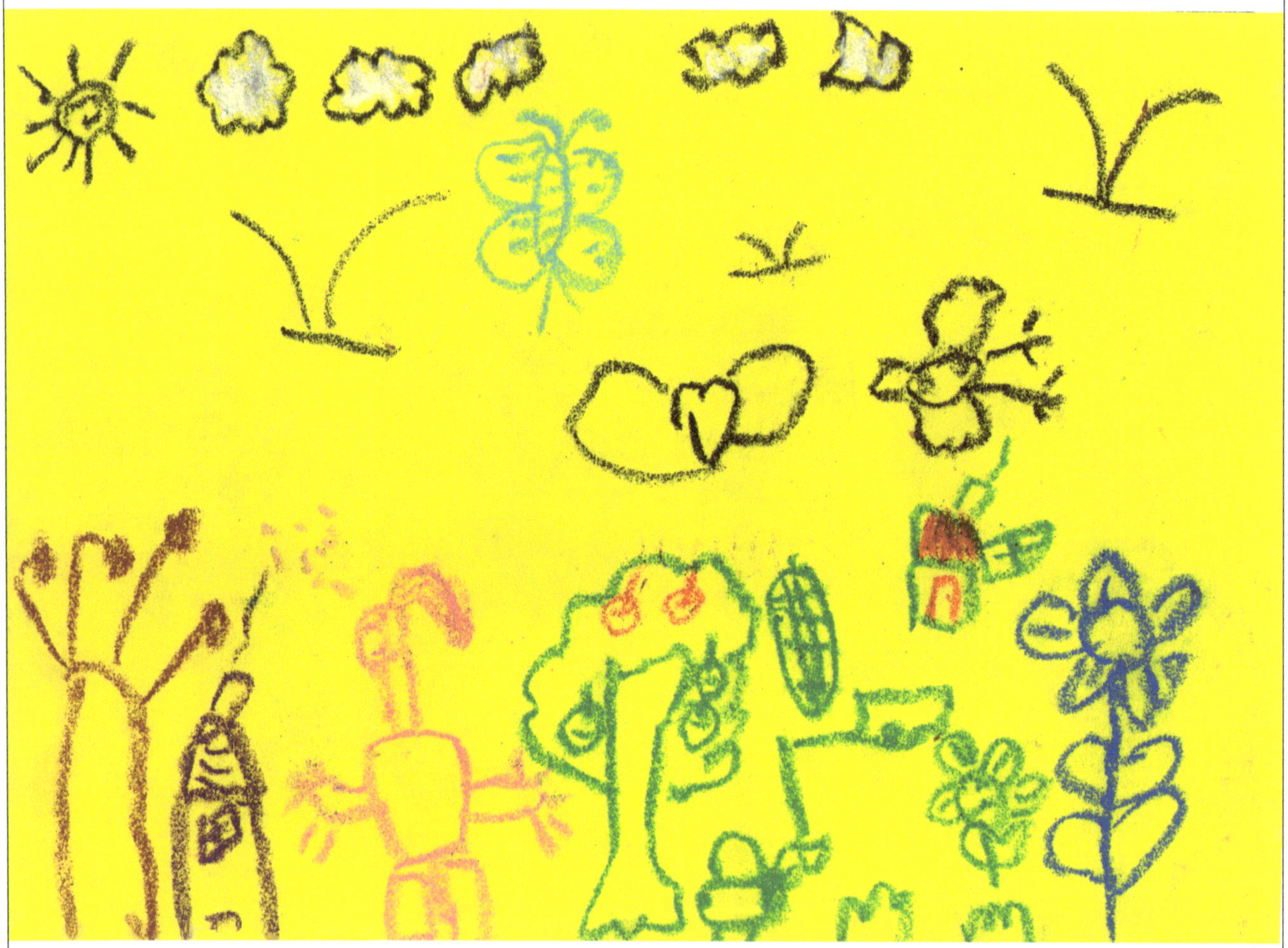

米奇的家（Mickey's home）

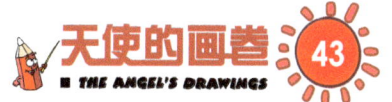

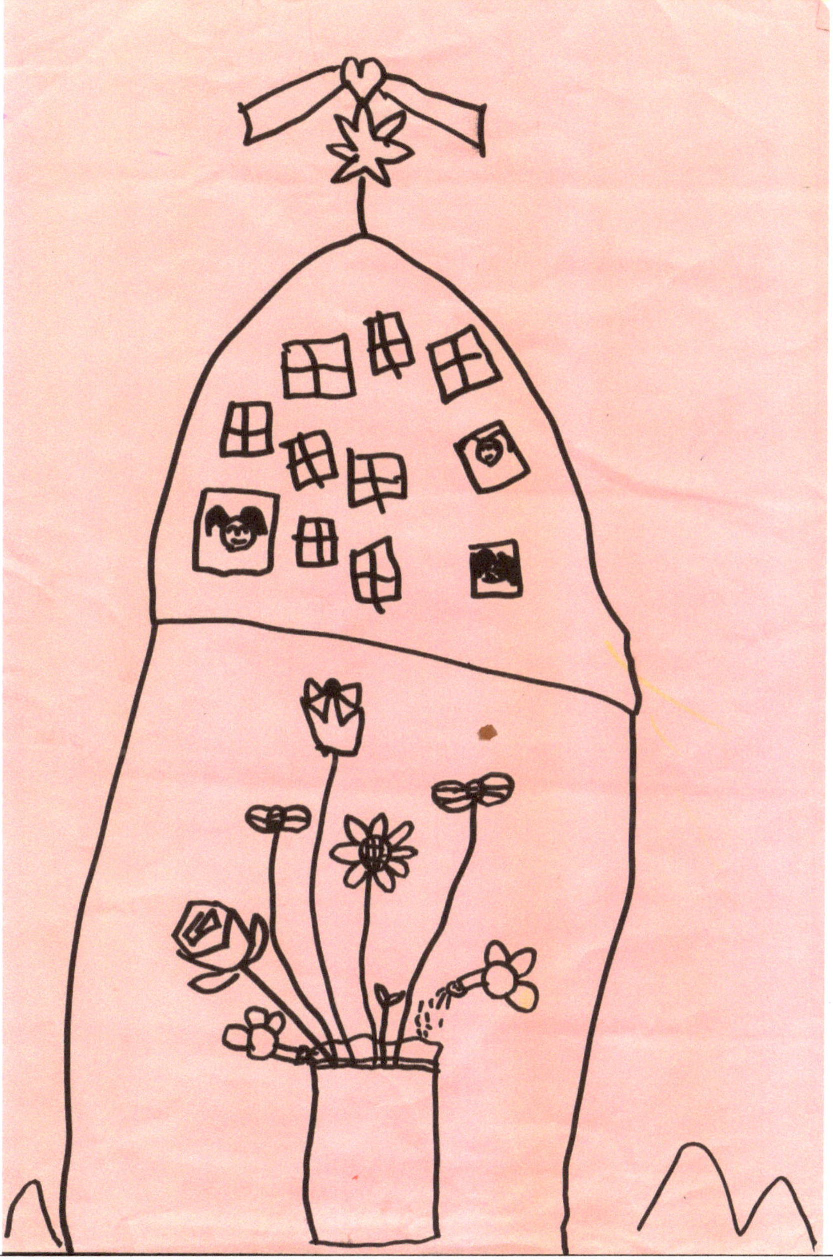

花房（A conservatory）

第三部分斑斓

Chapter Three: Colorfulness

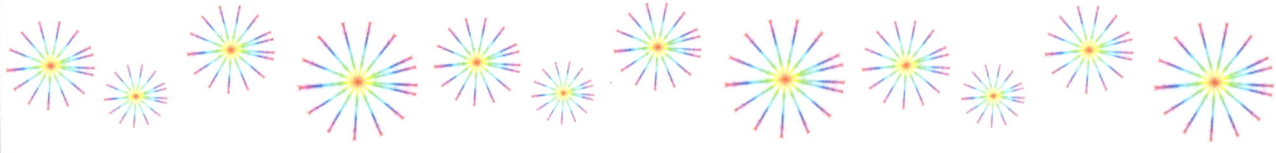

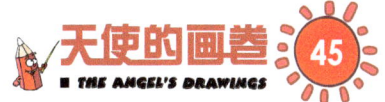

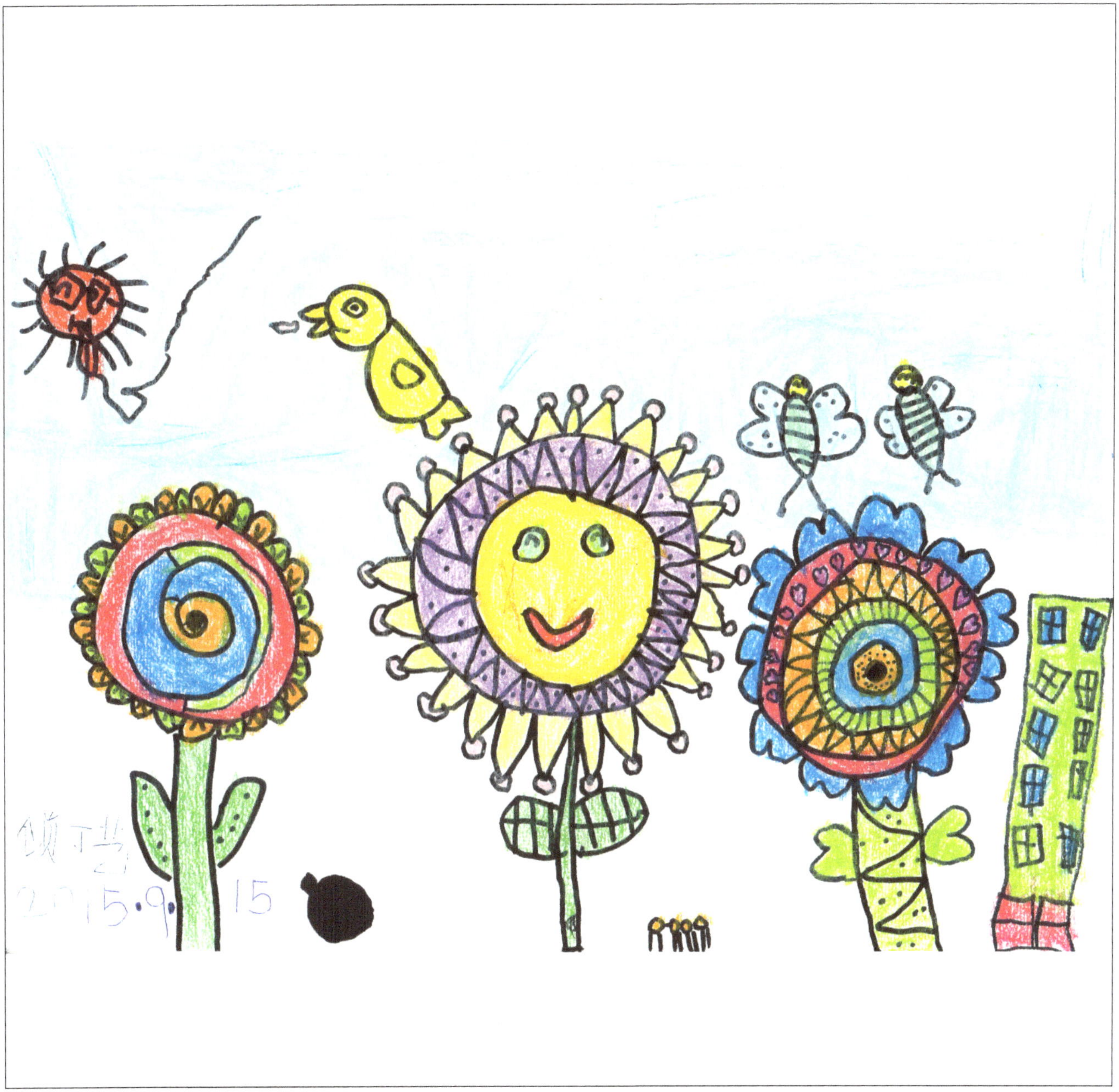

花园（The garden）

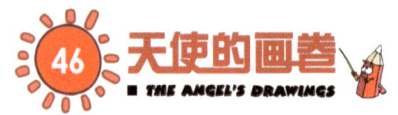

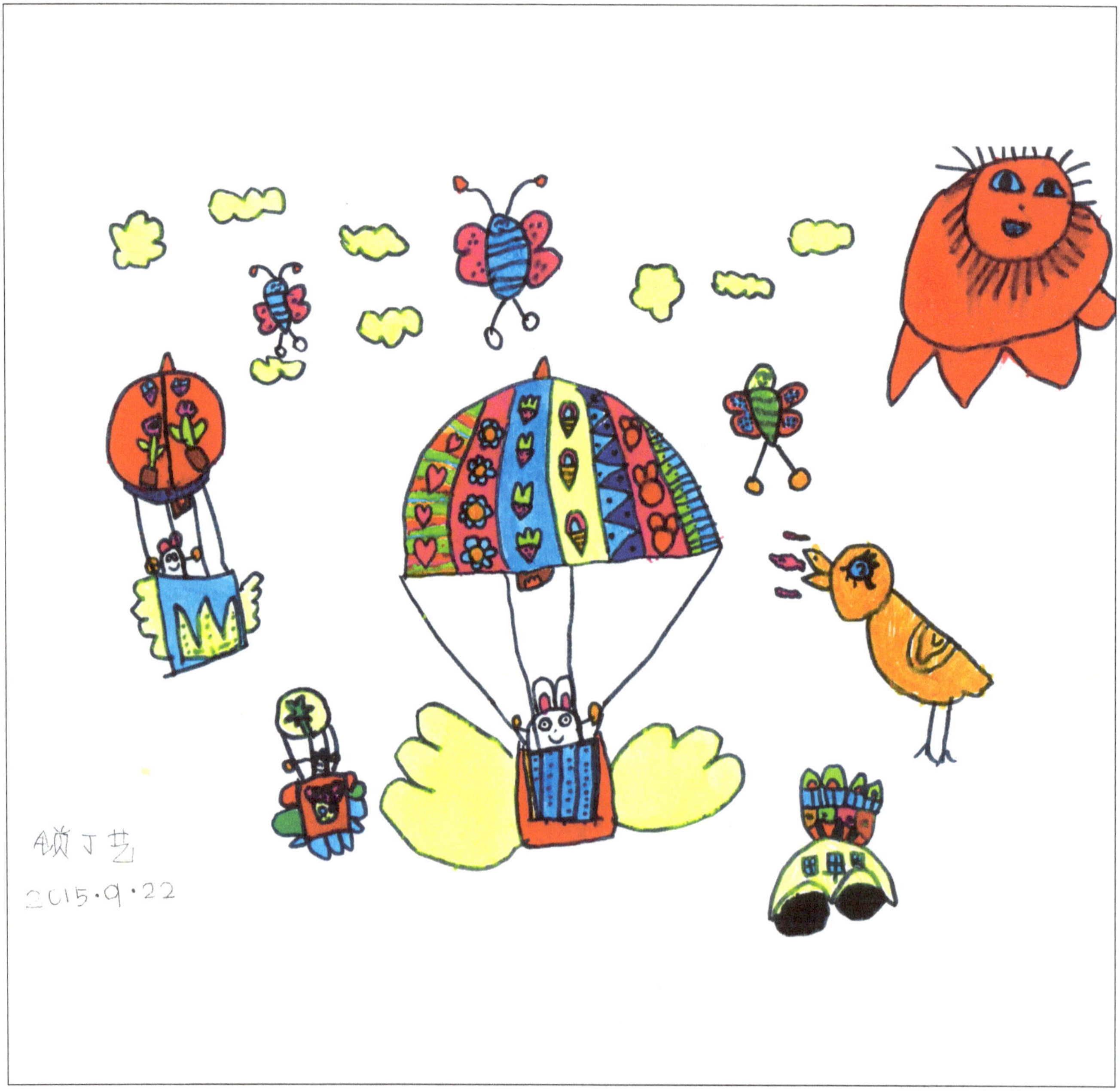

空中飞翔（Flying in the air）

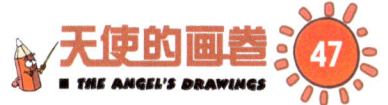

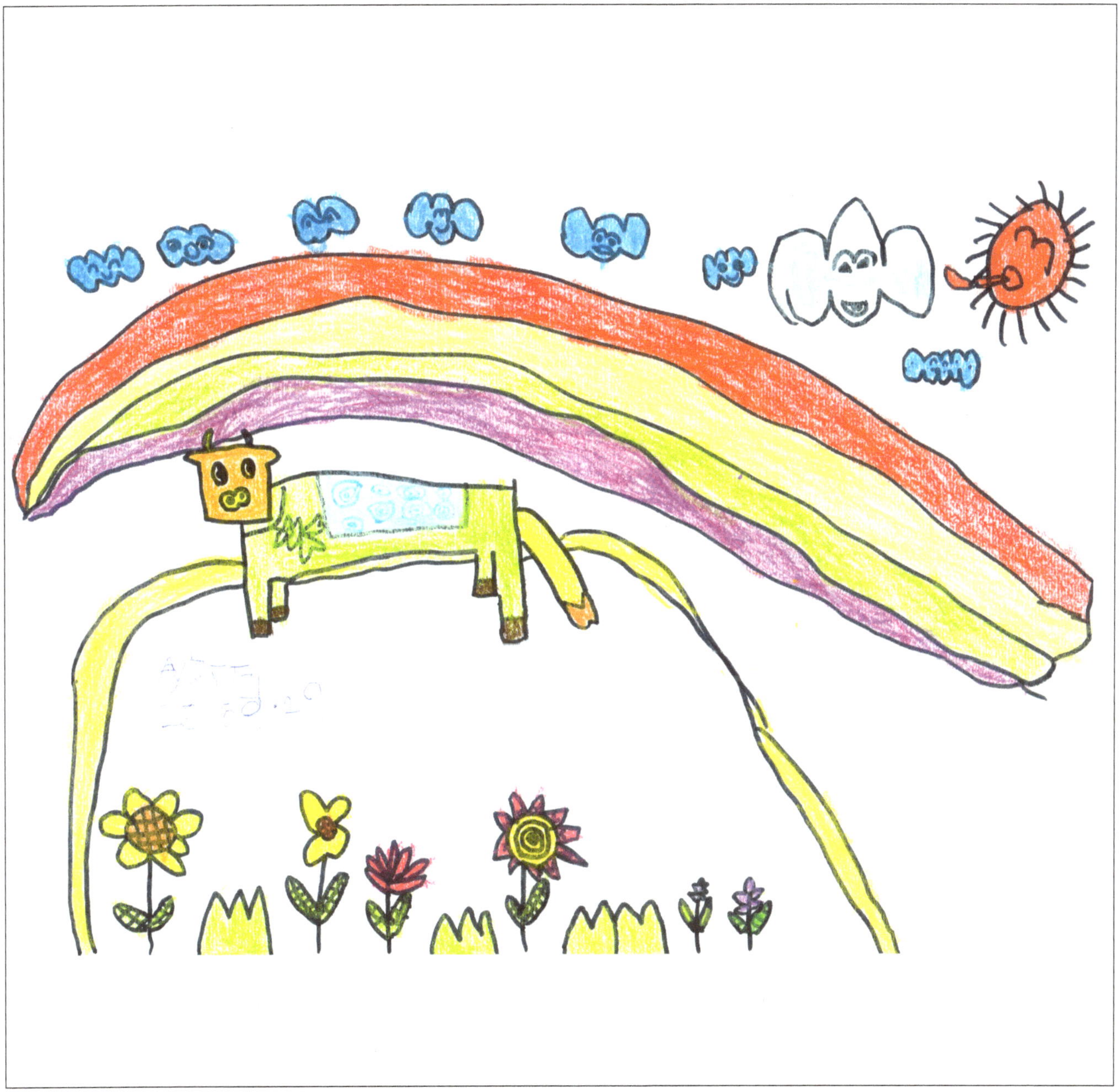

草原（The grassland）

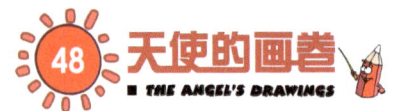

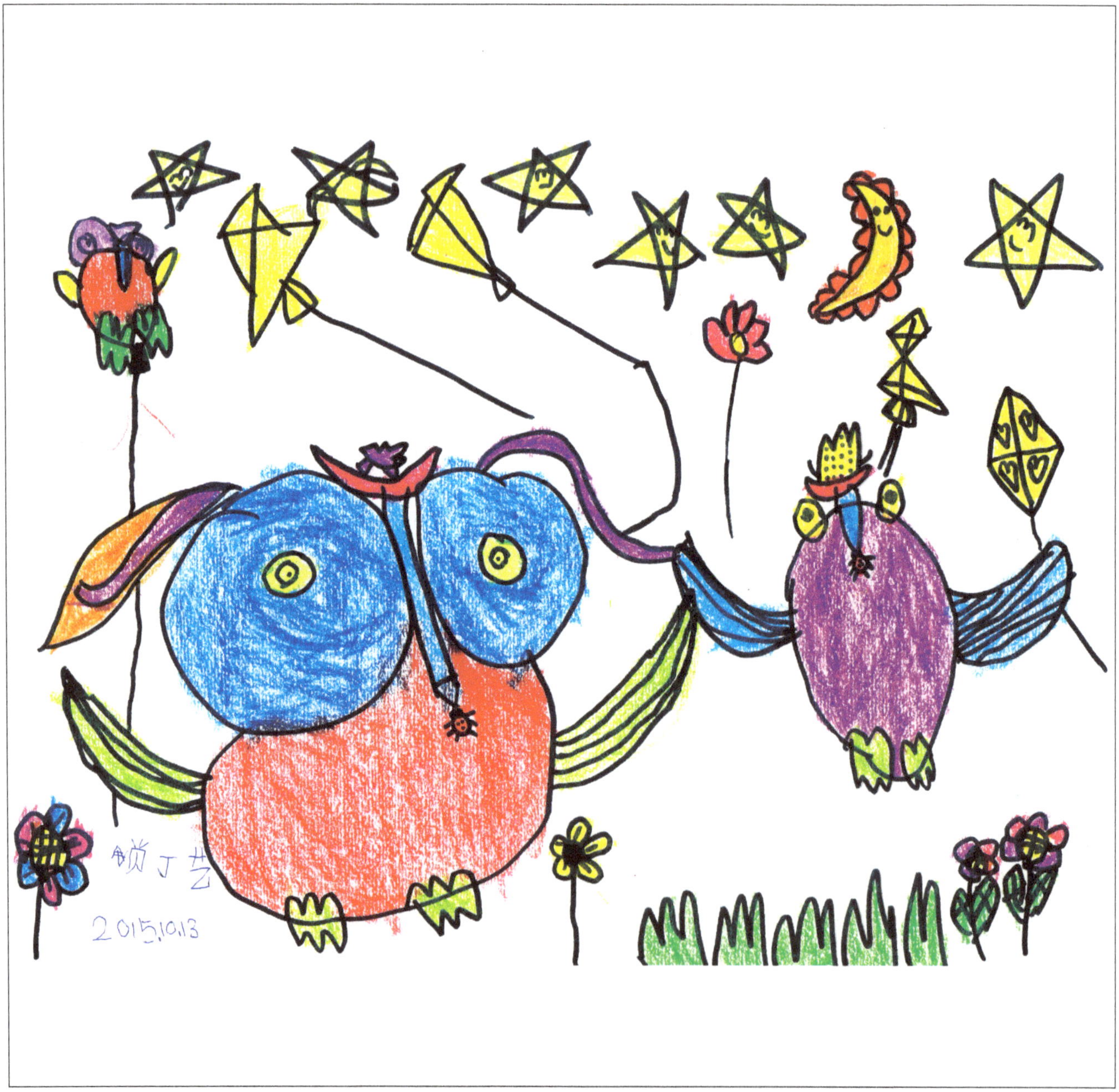

黑夜（The night）

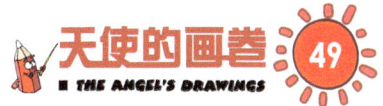

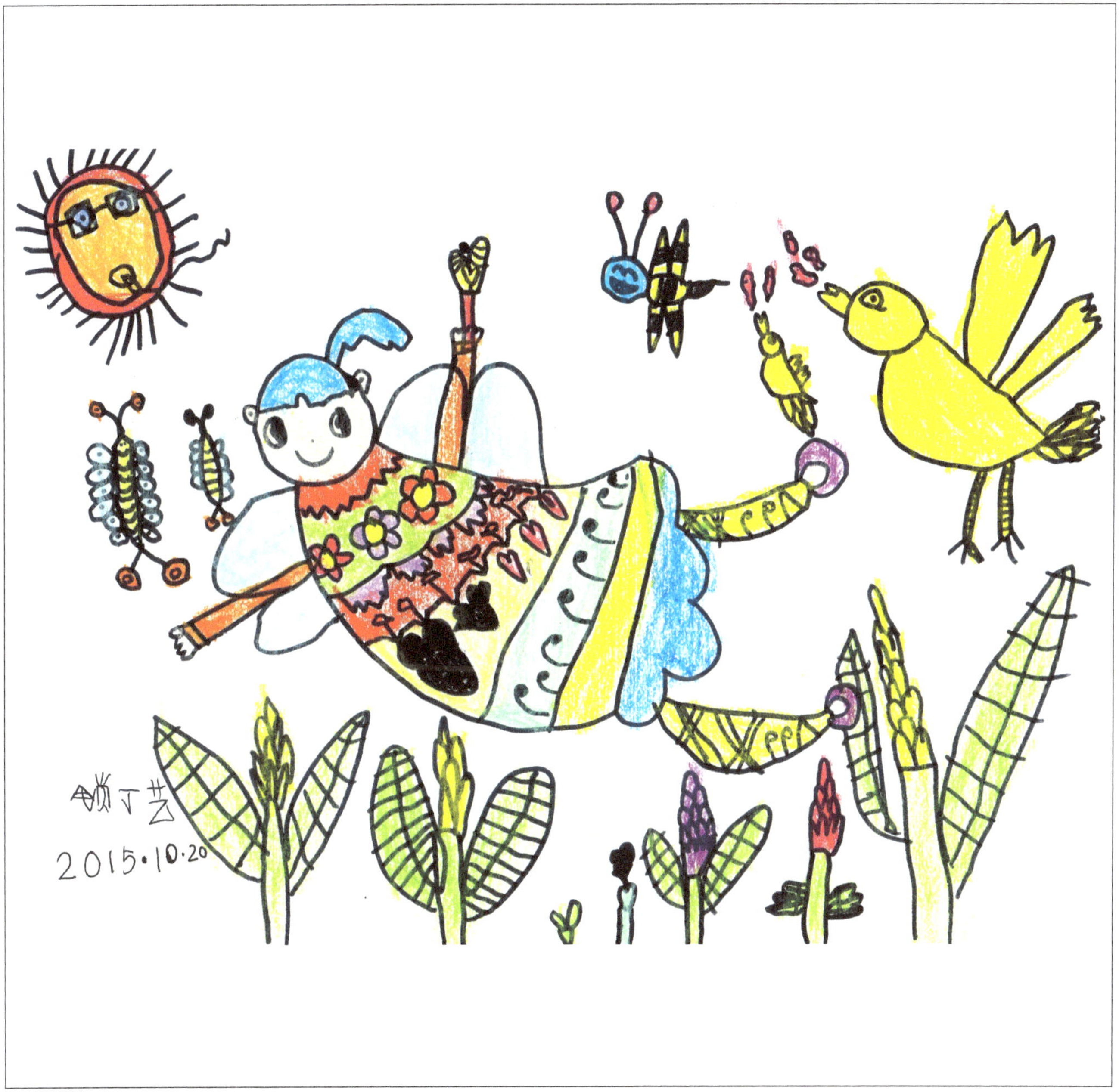

飞翔季节（The season of flying）

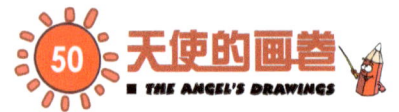

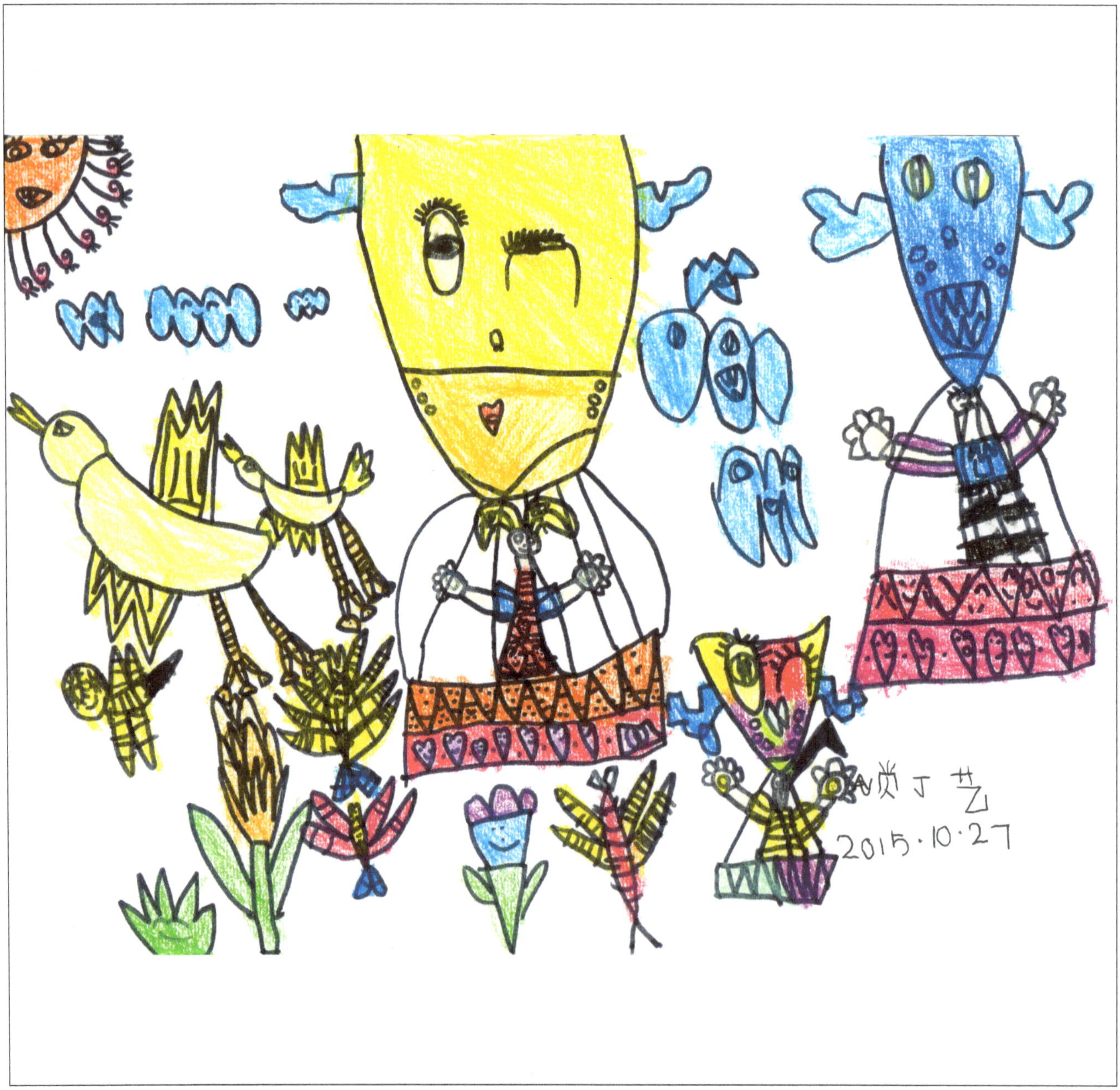

蓝色空间（Blue space）

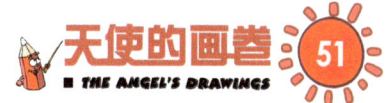

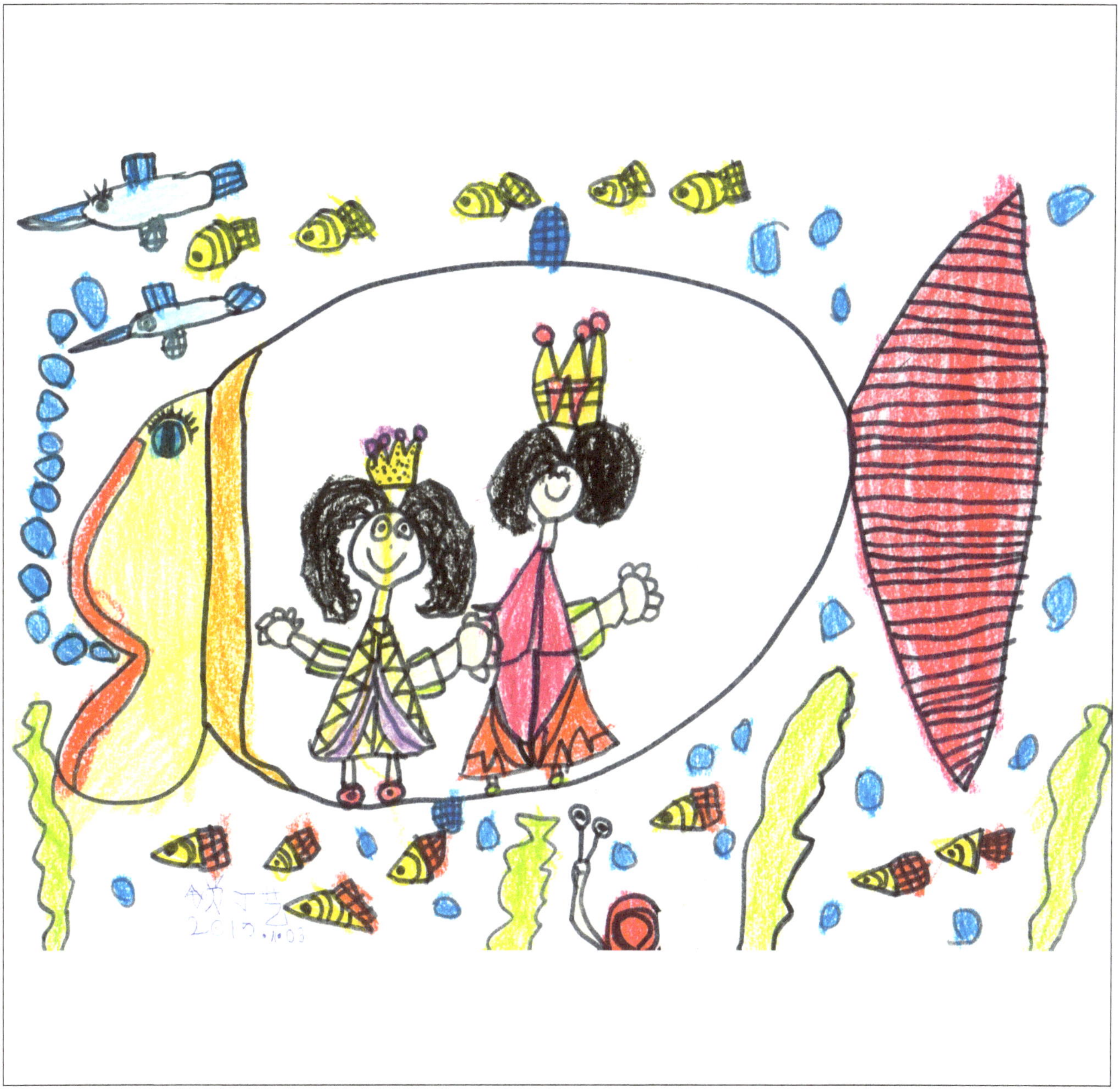

大海（The sea）

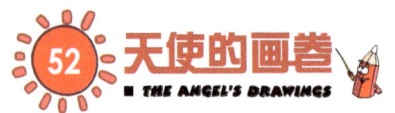

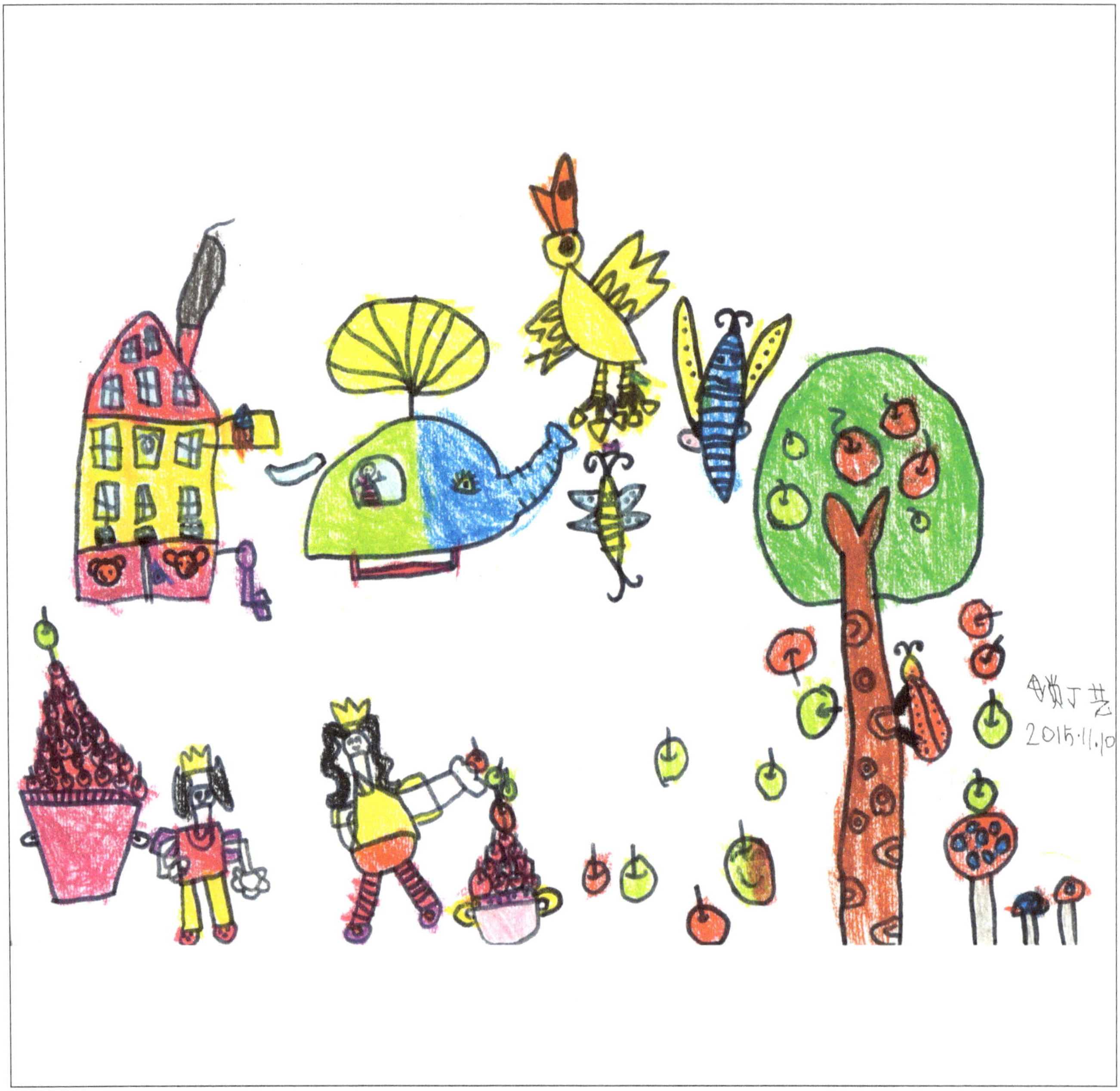

摘苹果大游行（Parade for apple picking）

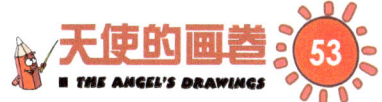
2015.11.7

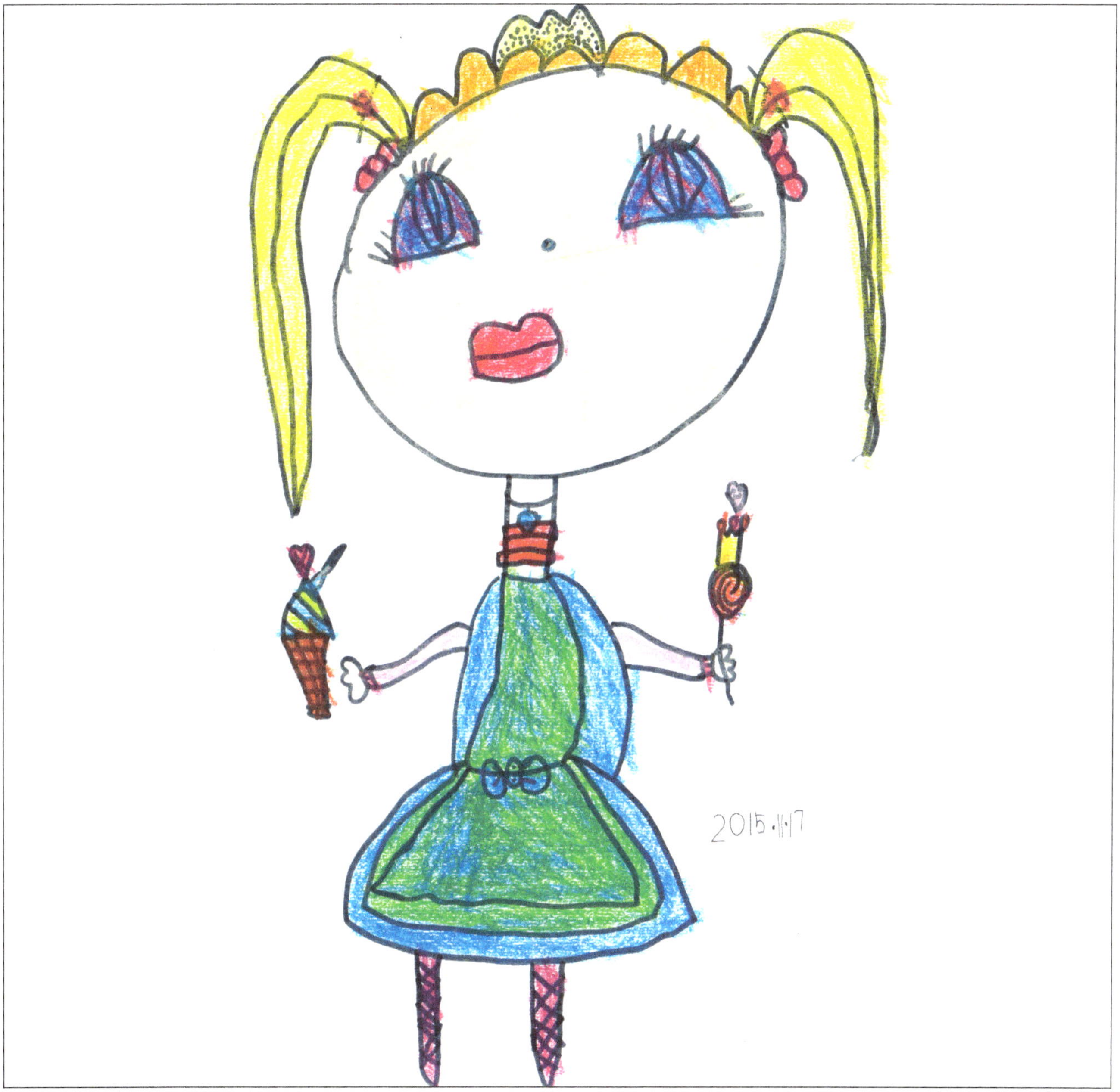

外国小姑娘（A little girl from foreign country）

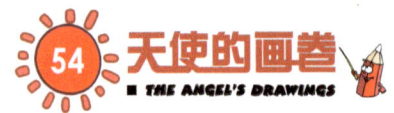

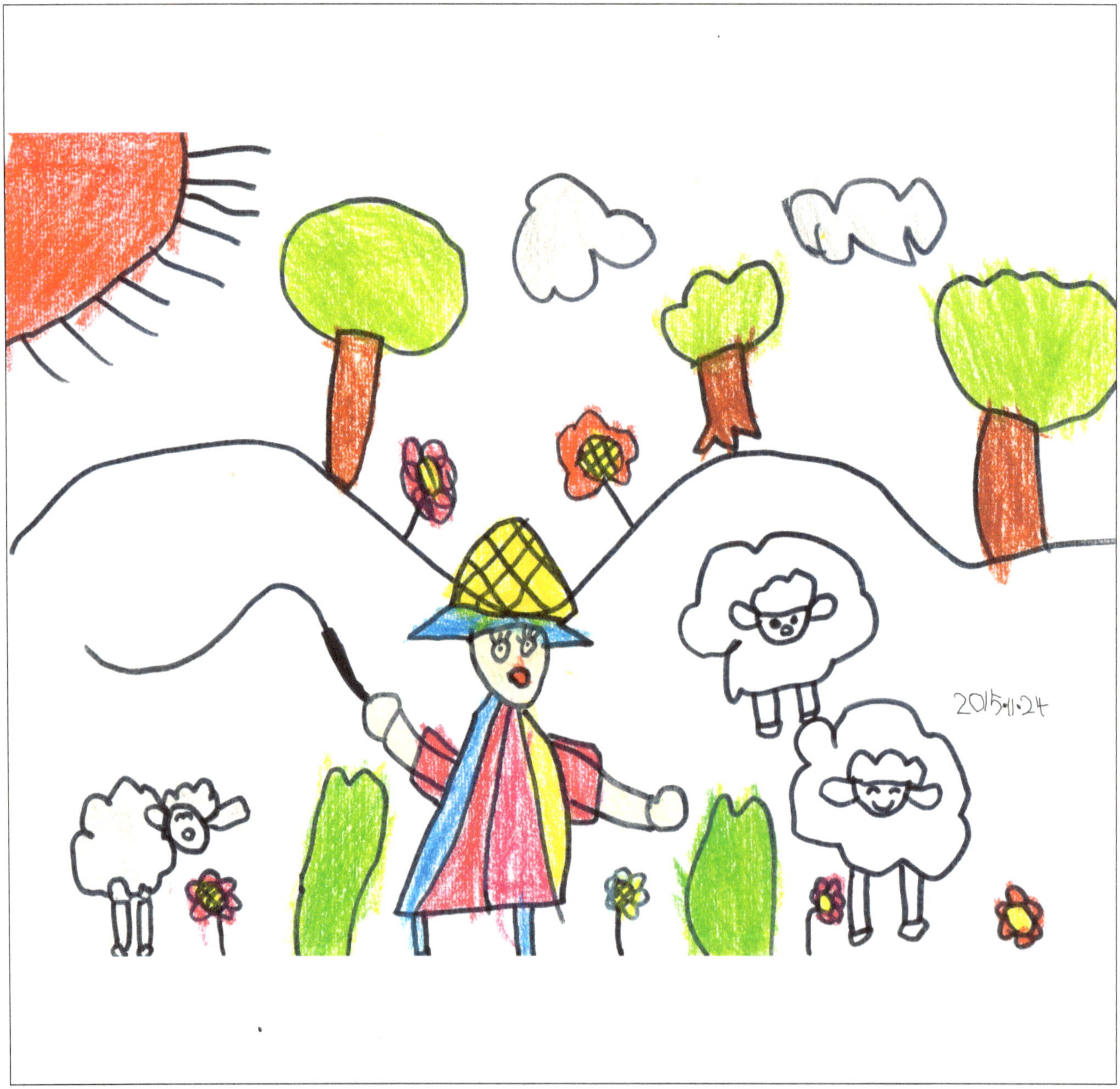

羊村（A sheep village）

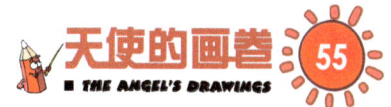

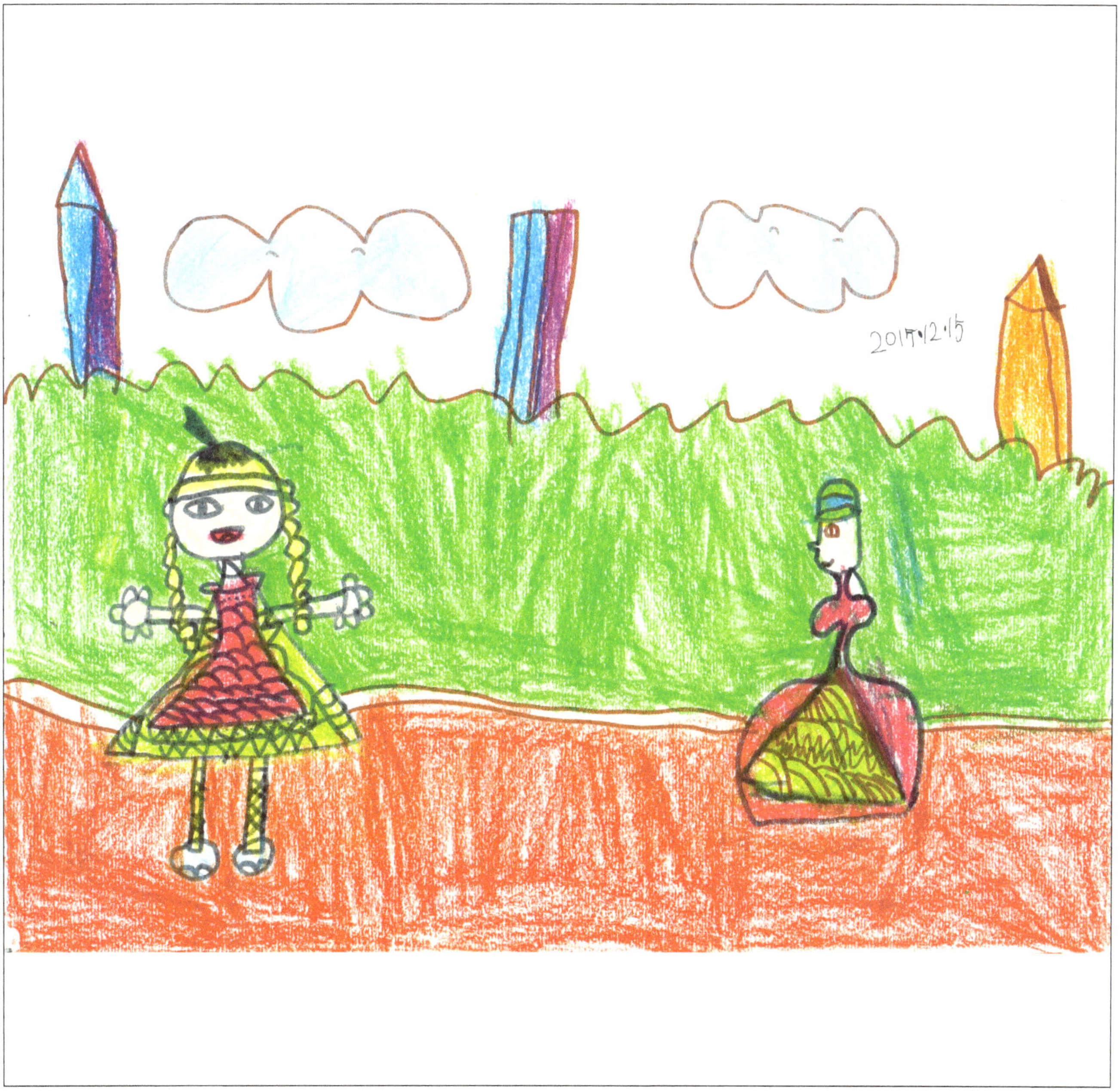

2019.12.15

放学回家路上（On the way home）

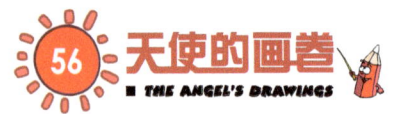

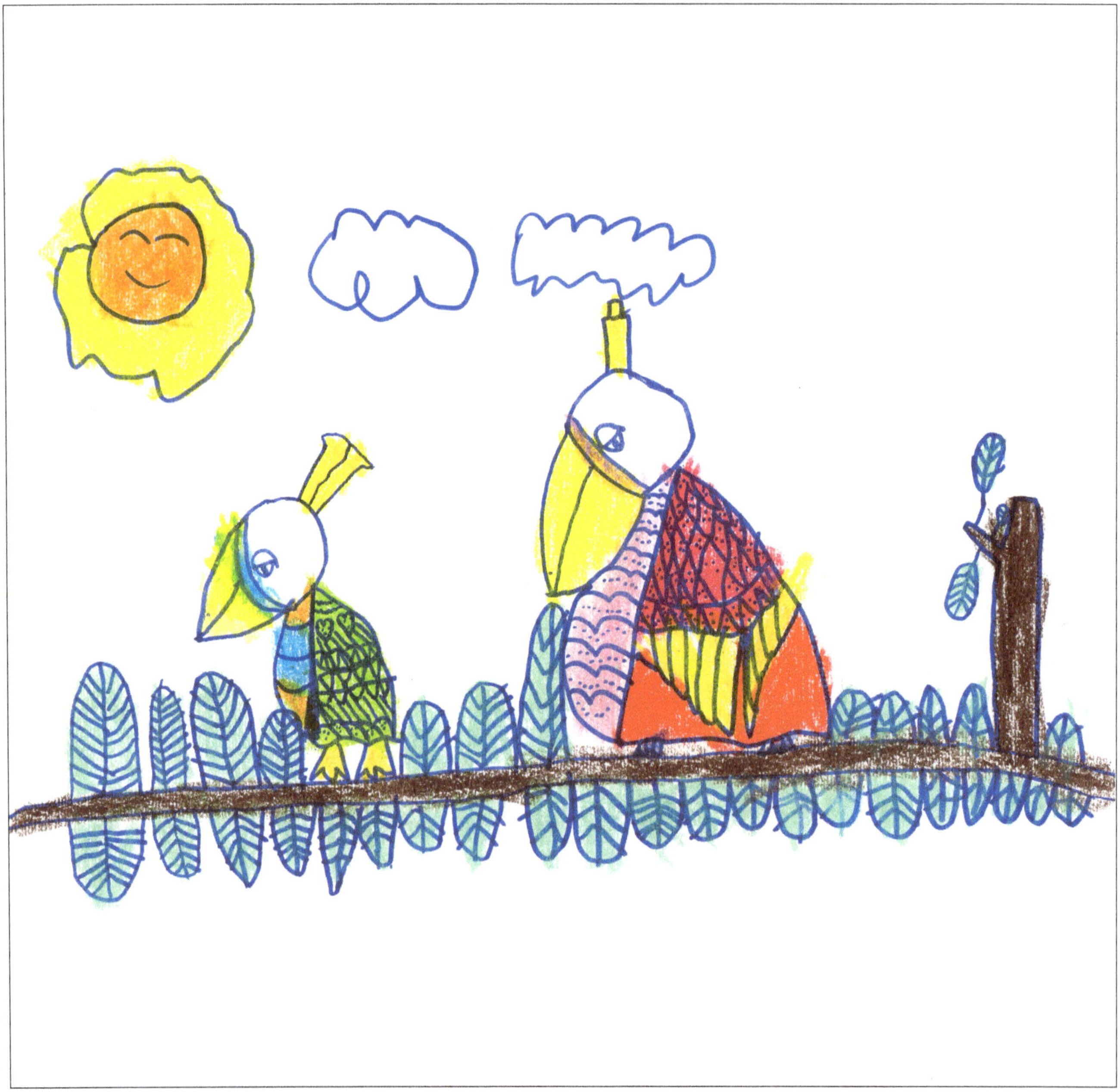

小鹦鹉和妈妈（A little parrot and her mom）

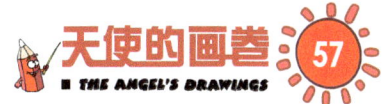

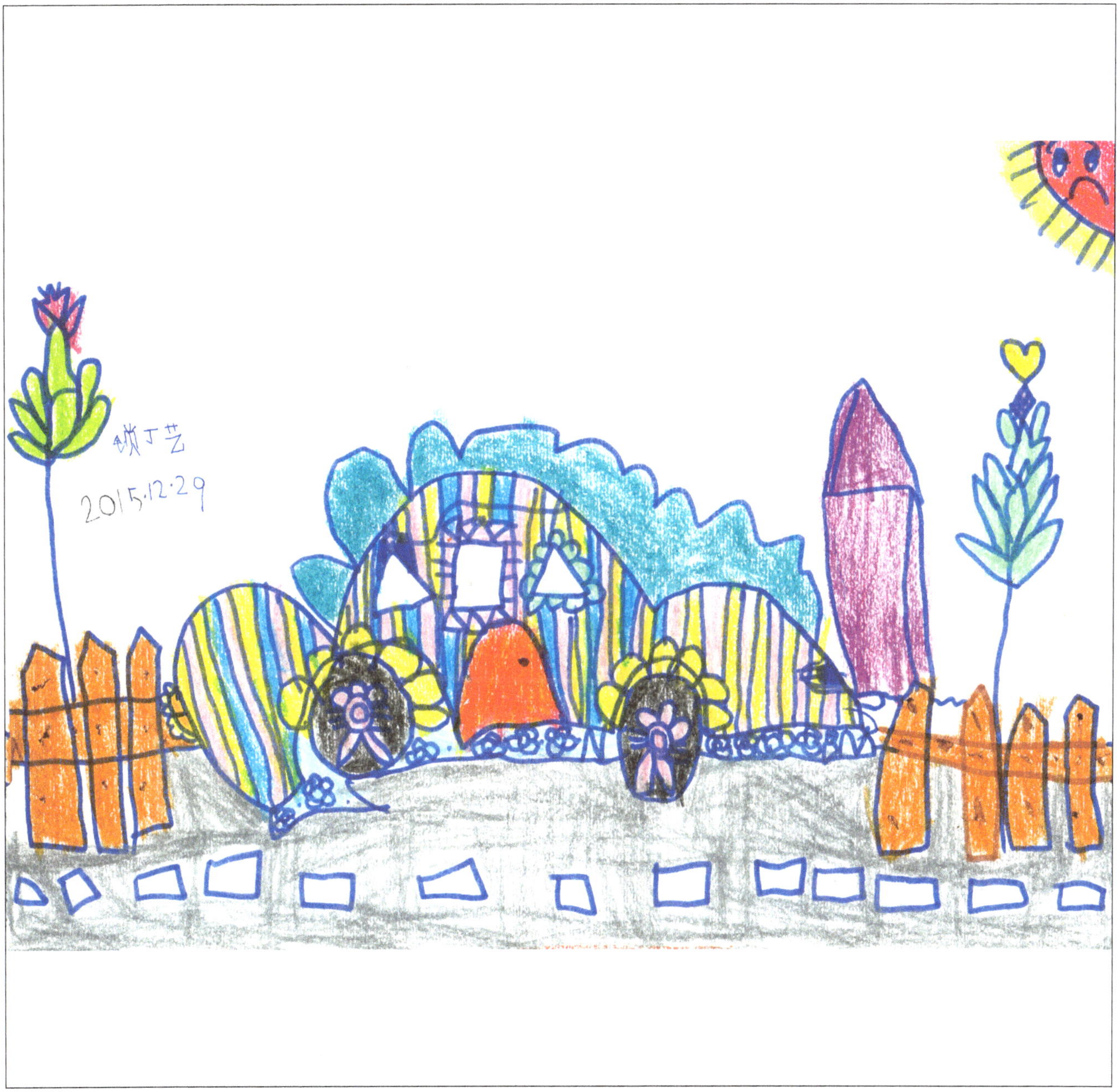

小汽车 "嘀嘀嘀"（Talking cars）

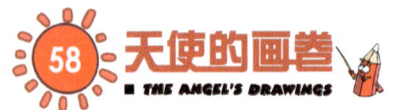

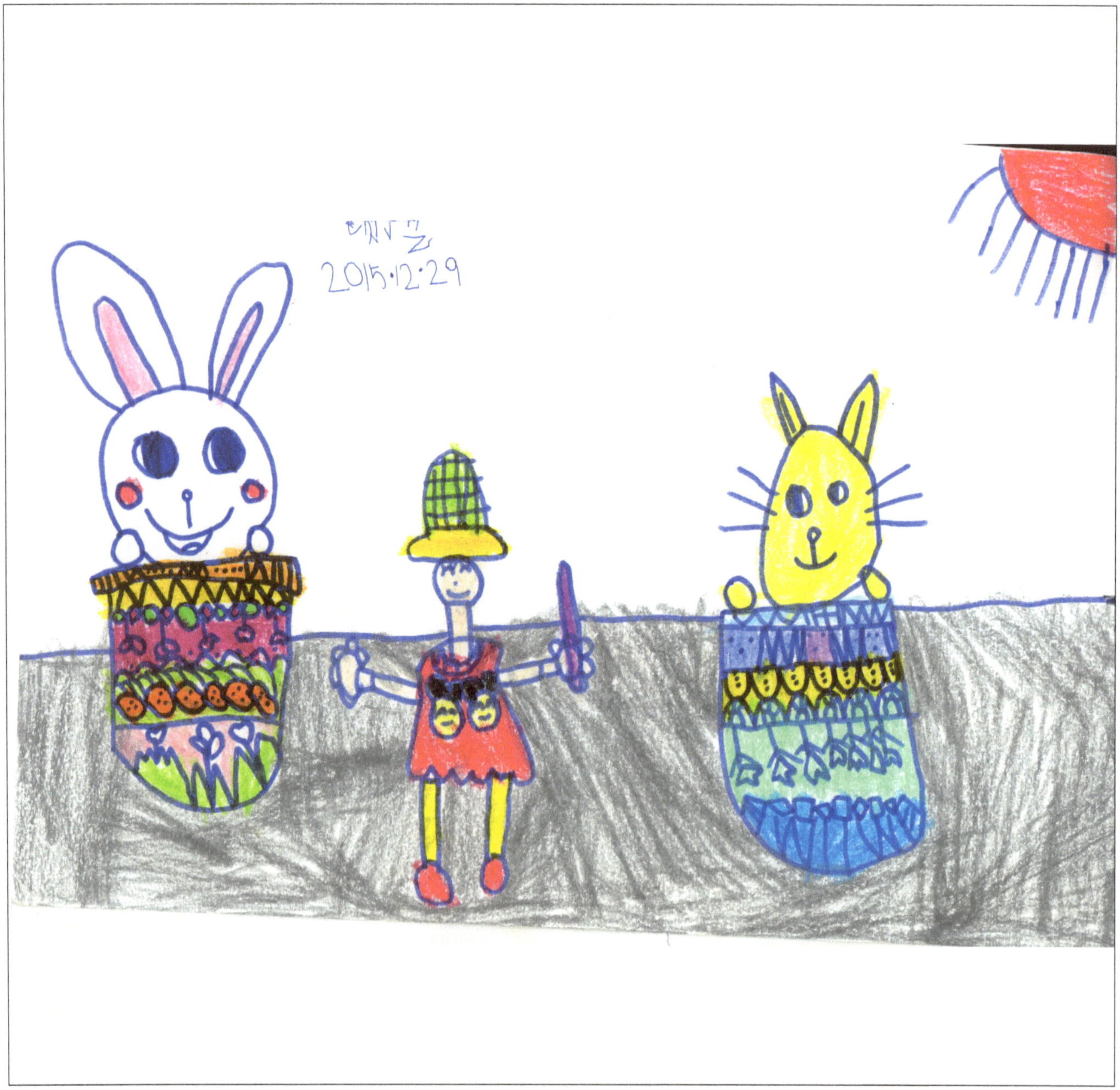

魔术师"变变变"（A magician doing his magics）

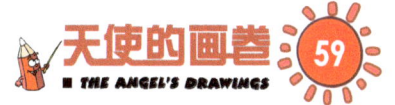

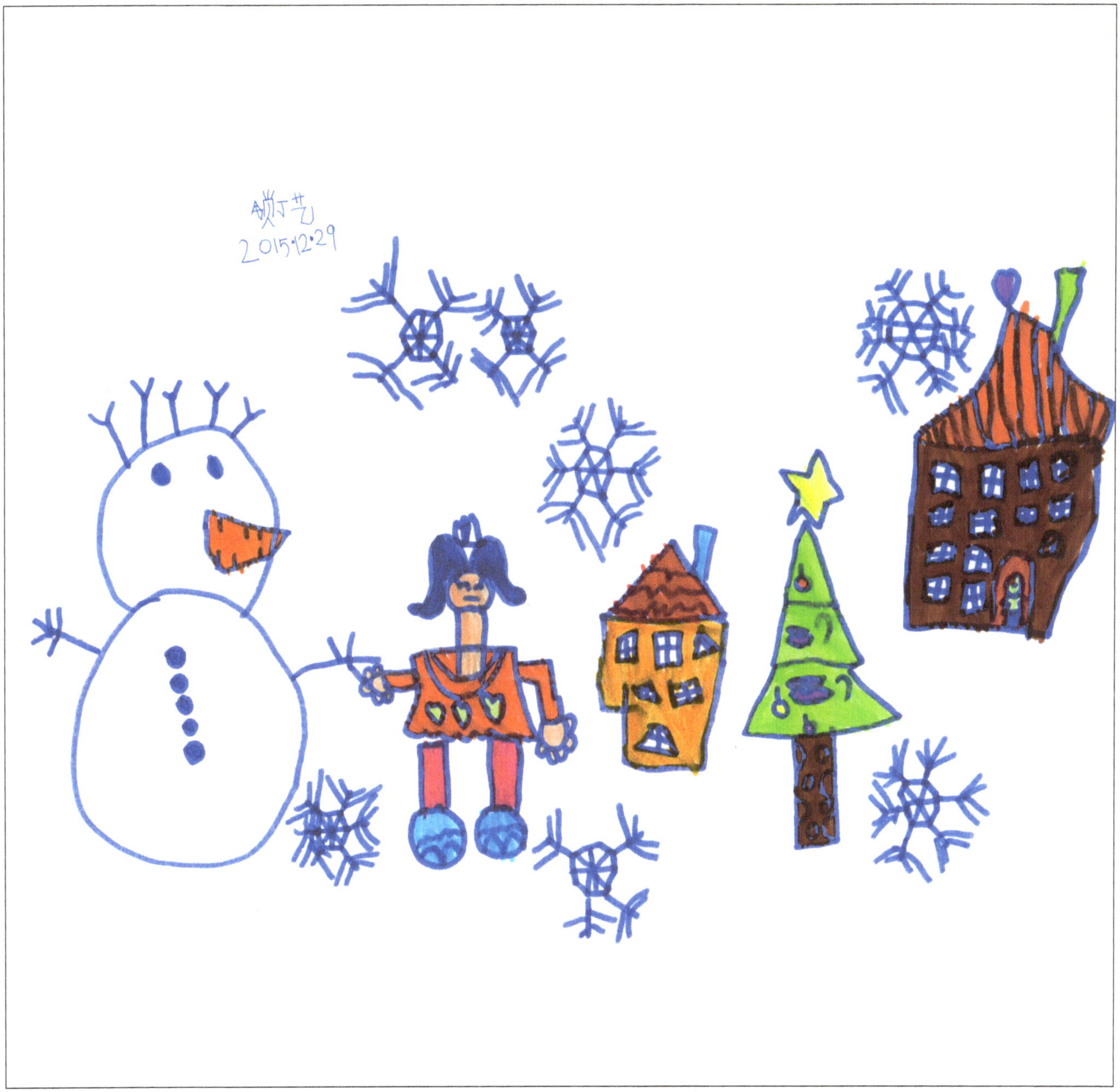

赖灯艺
2015·12·29

圣诞节（Christmas）

第四部分 绚丽

Chapter Four: Beauty

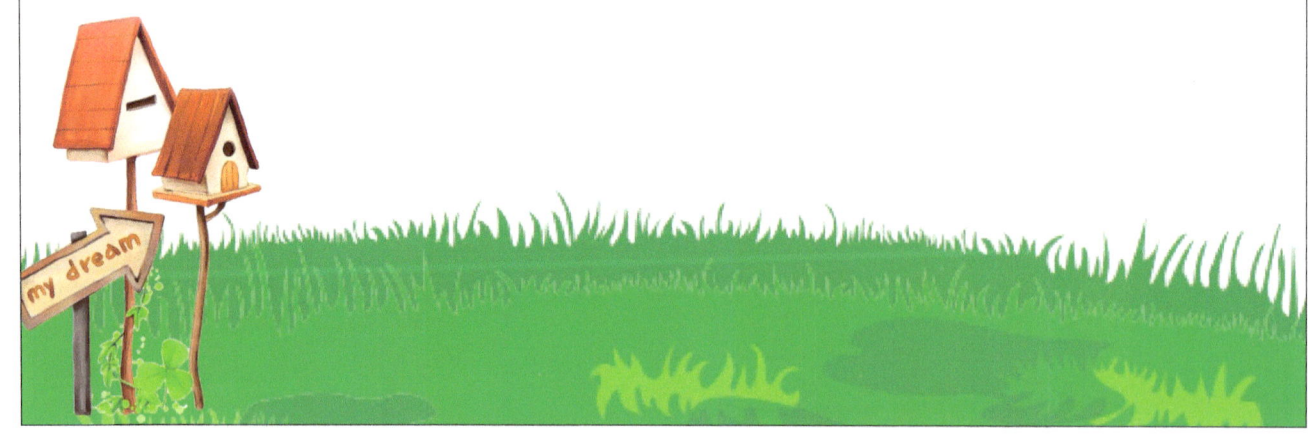

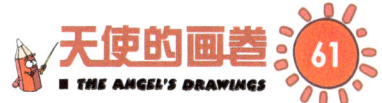

祝姥姥新年快乐! 丁艺 收到姥姥的包裹啦 丁丁非常感动, 读了姥姥的来信, 这是一份我收到的最珍贵的礼物, 我已经把它收藏到了我的宝藏箱里。我非常喜欢姥姥寄给我的衣服

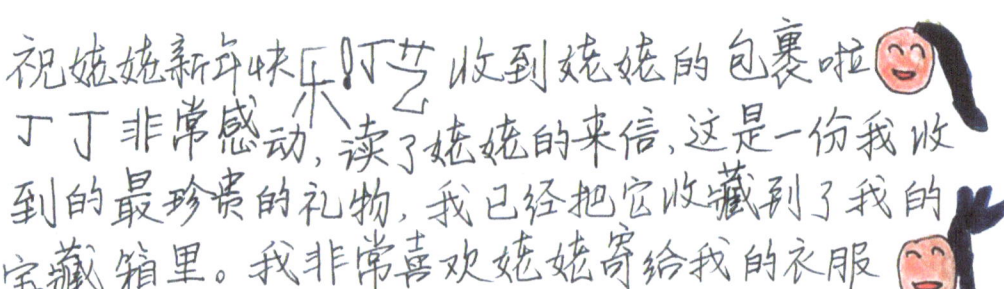

the words in the drawing were written

by Ding Ding′s mom

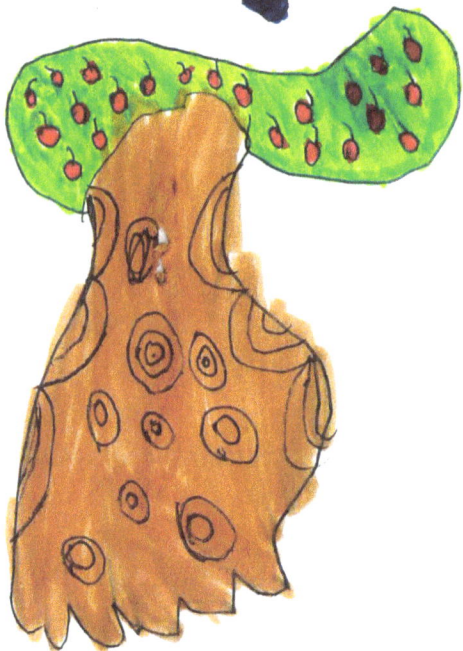

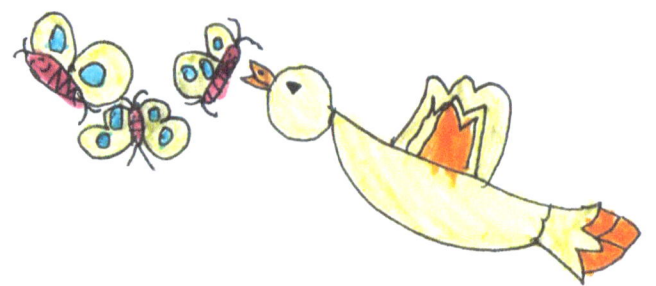

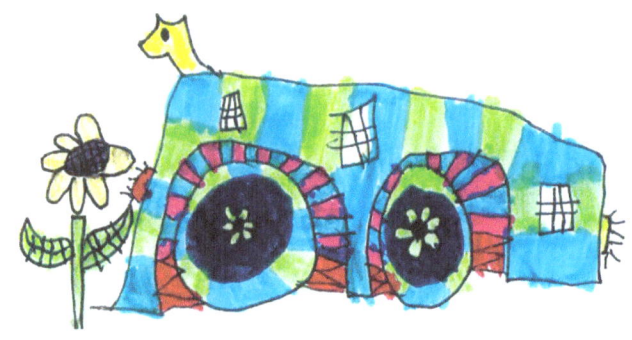

给姥姥的新年贺卡（A greeting card to grandpa）

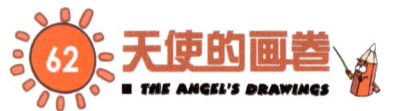

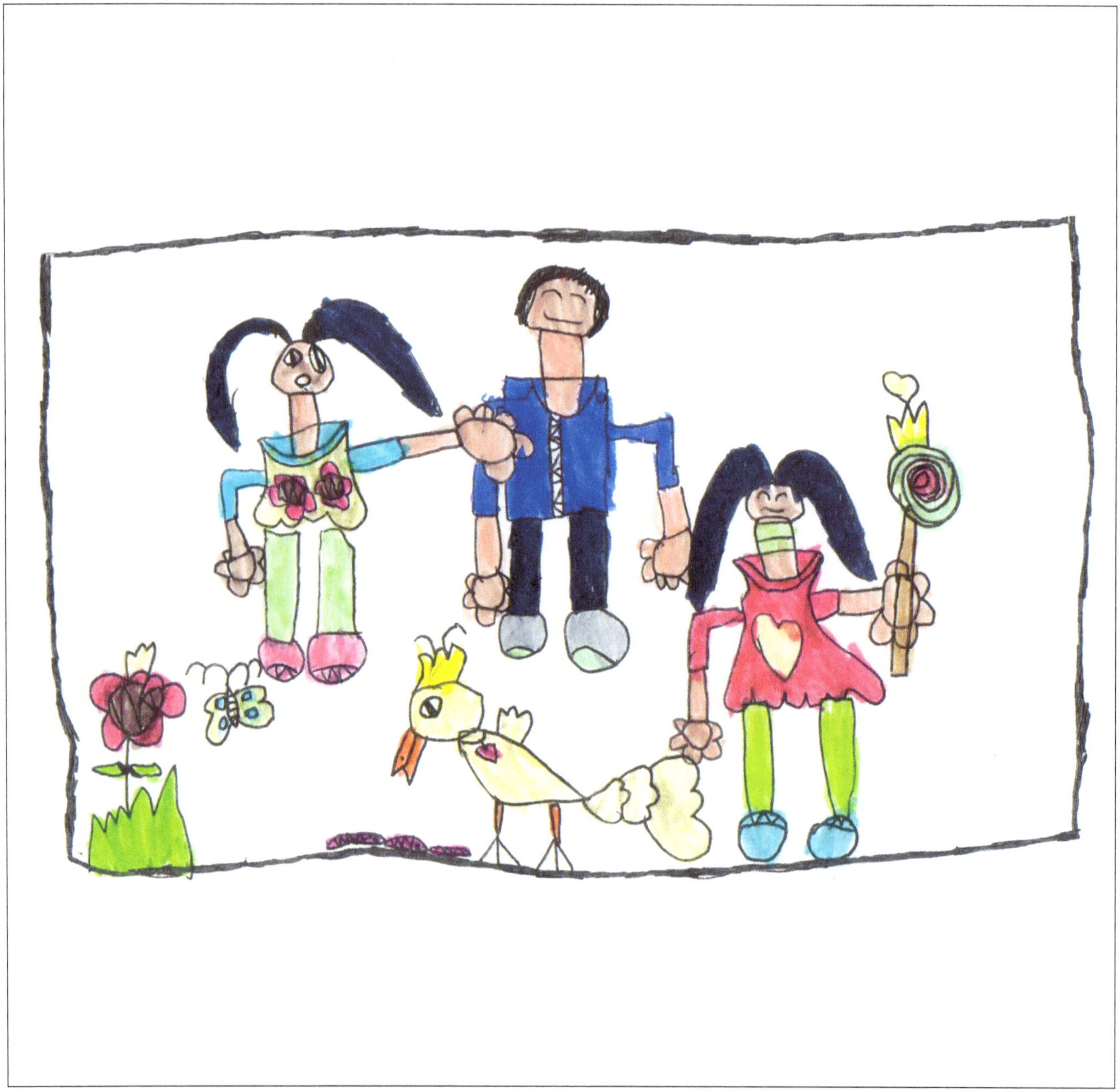

快乐的三口之家照片（A happy family of three）

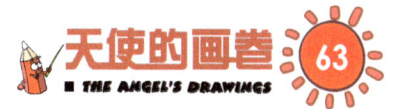

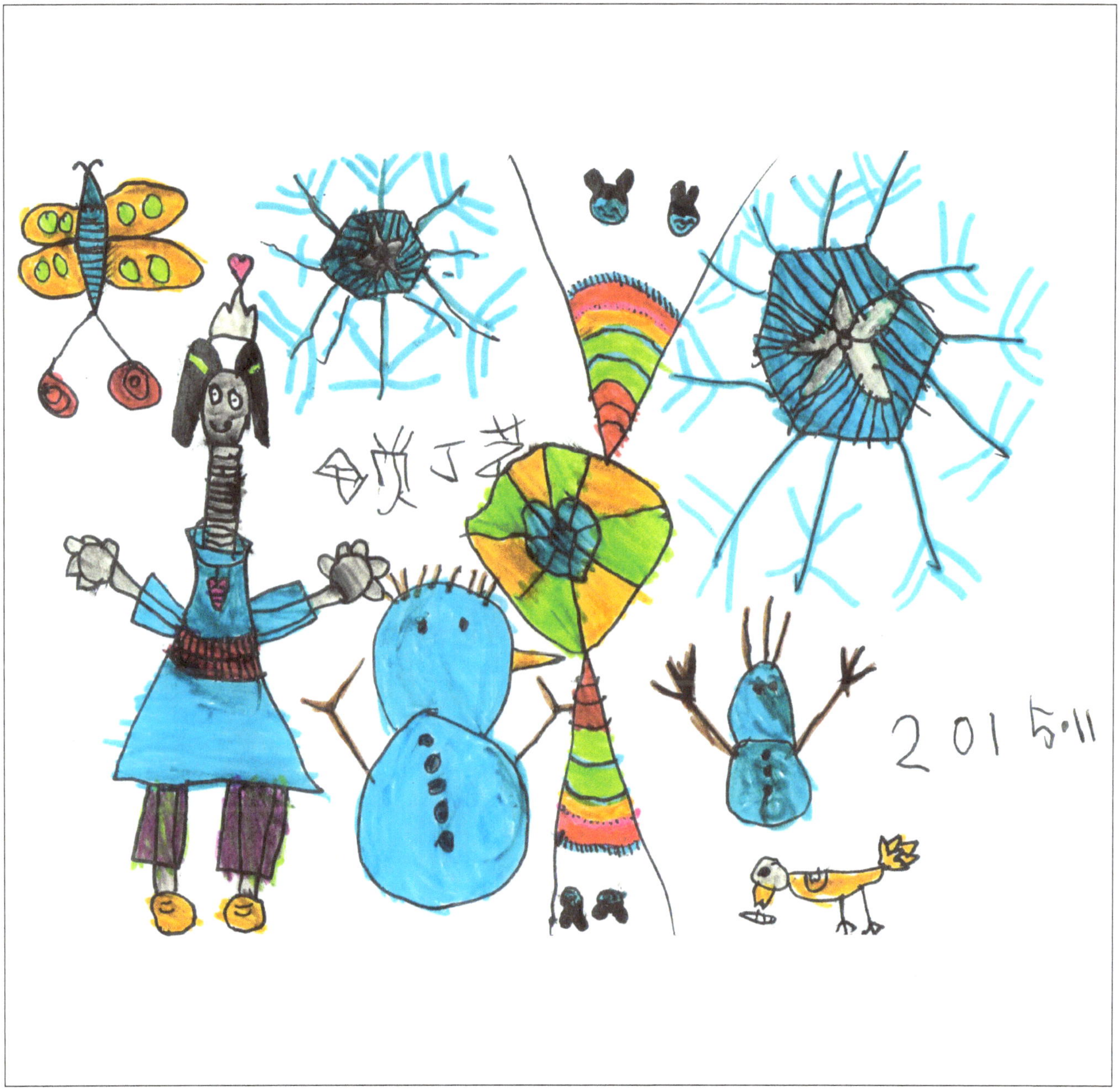

堆雪人（Marking a snowman）

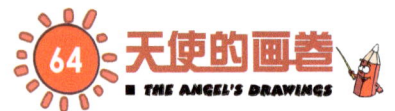

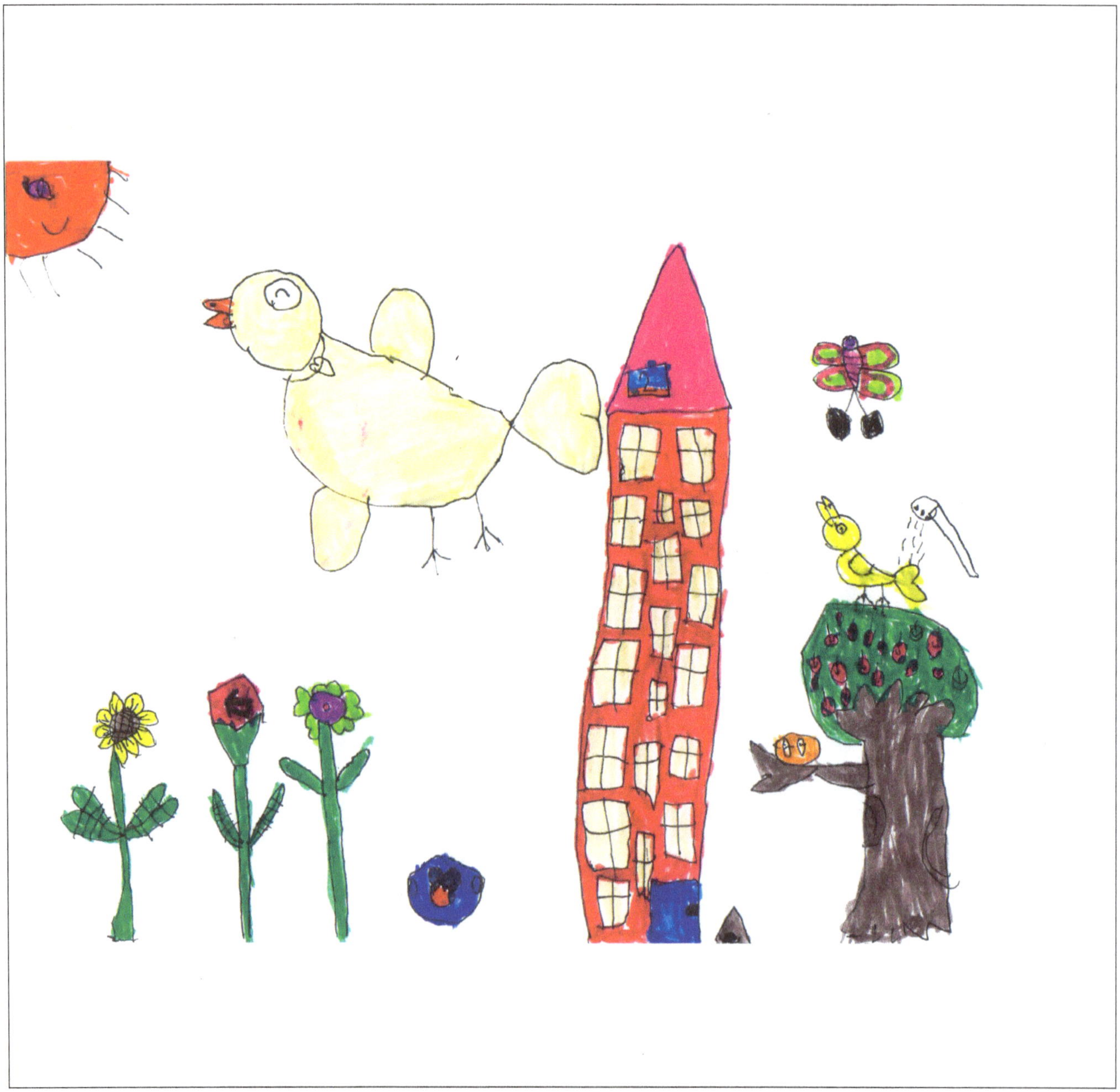

我的家（My home）

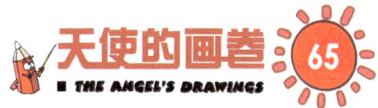

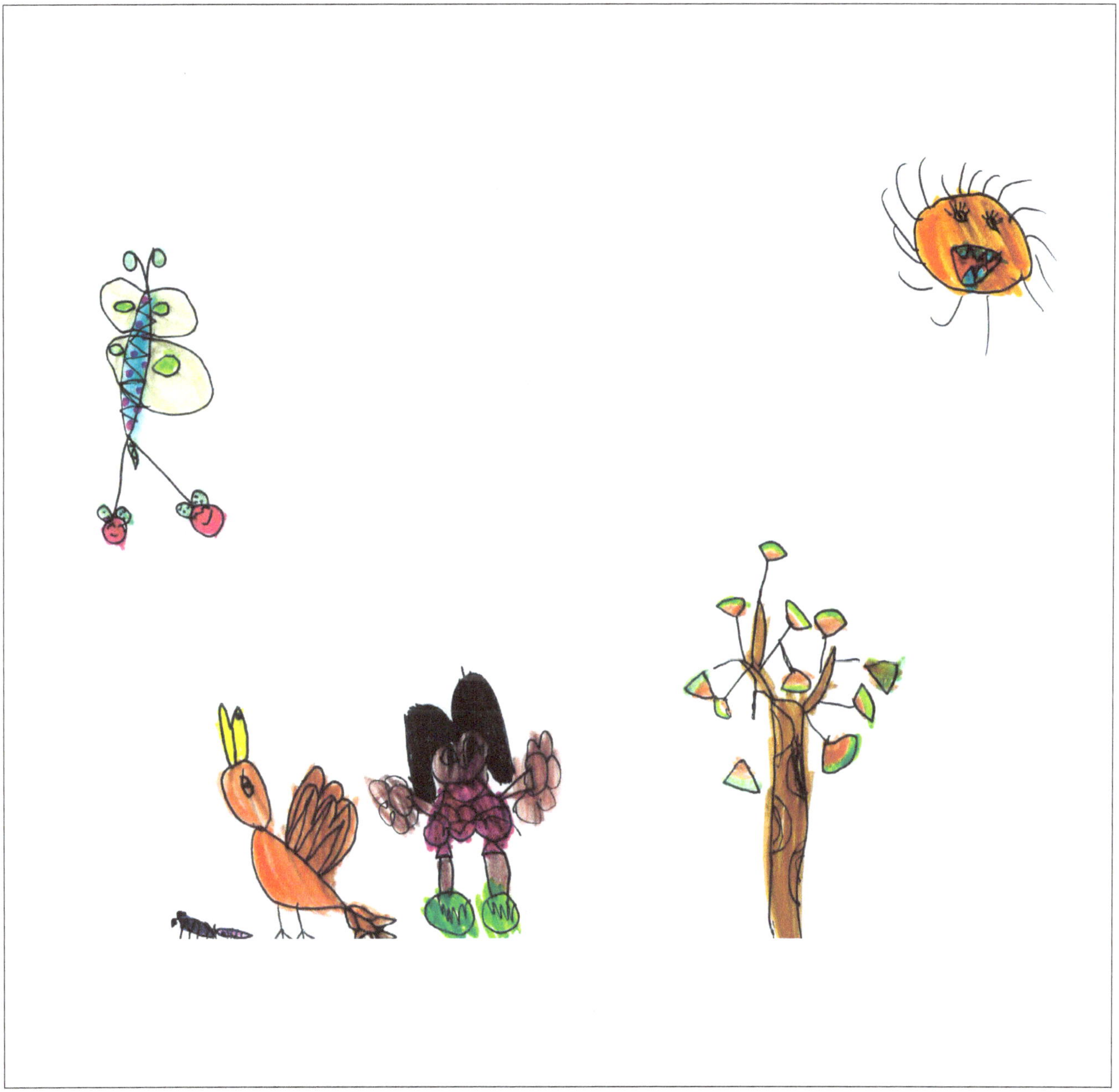

我爱大自然（I love the nature）

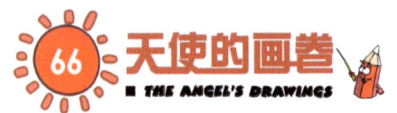
在蓝天下快乐生活（A happy life under blue sky）

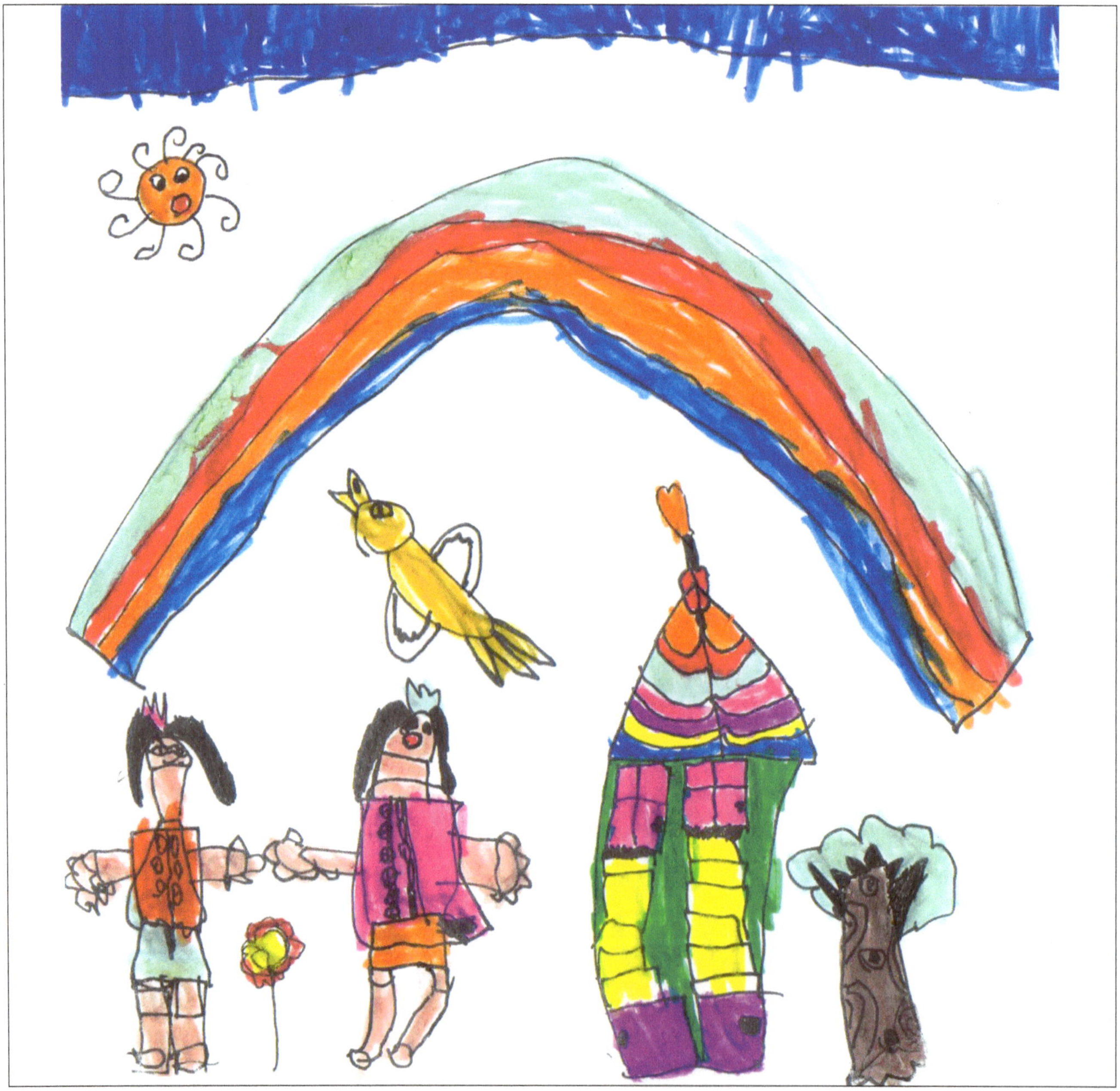

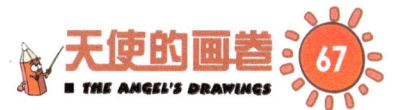
美丽大自然（The beautiful nature）

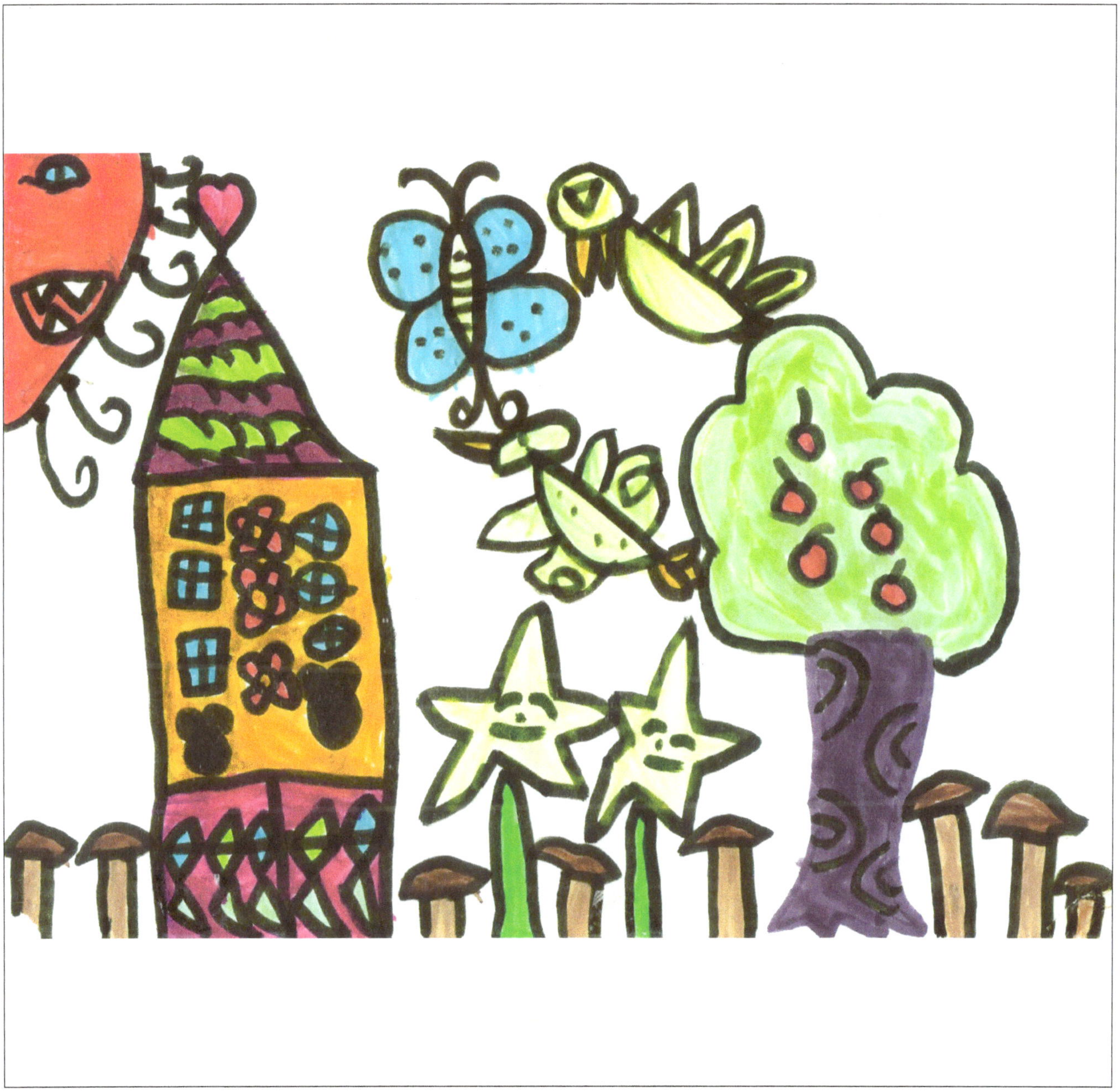

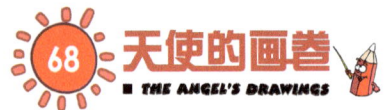

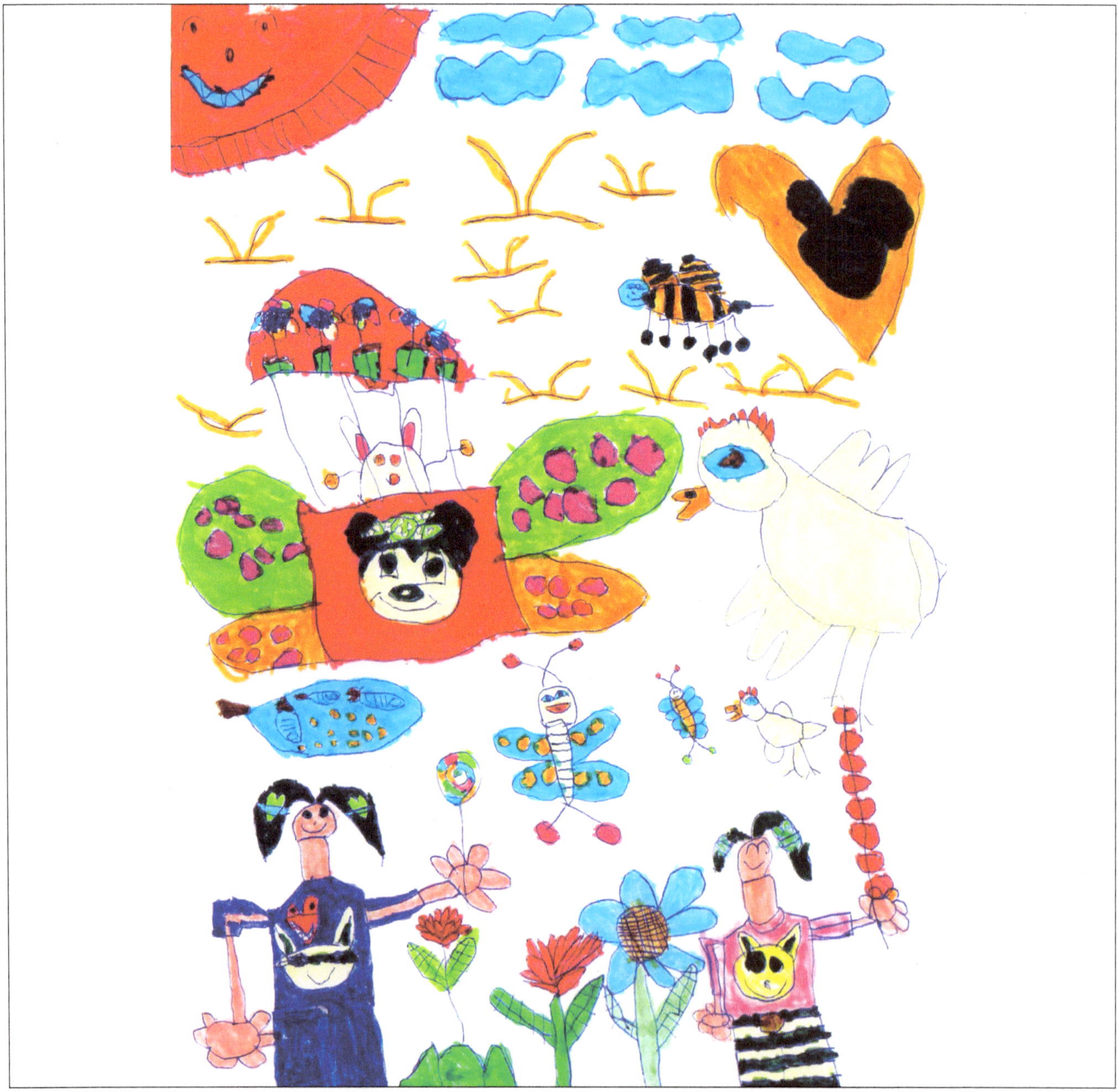

热气球旅行（Travel by hot air balloon）

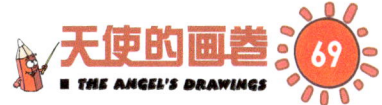

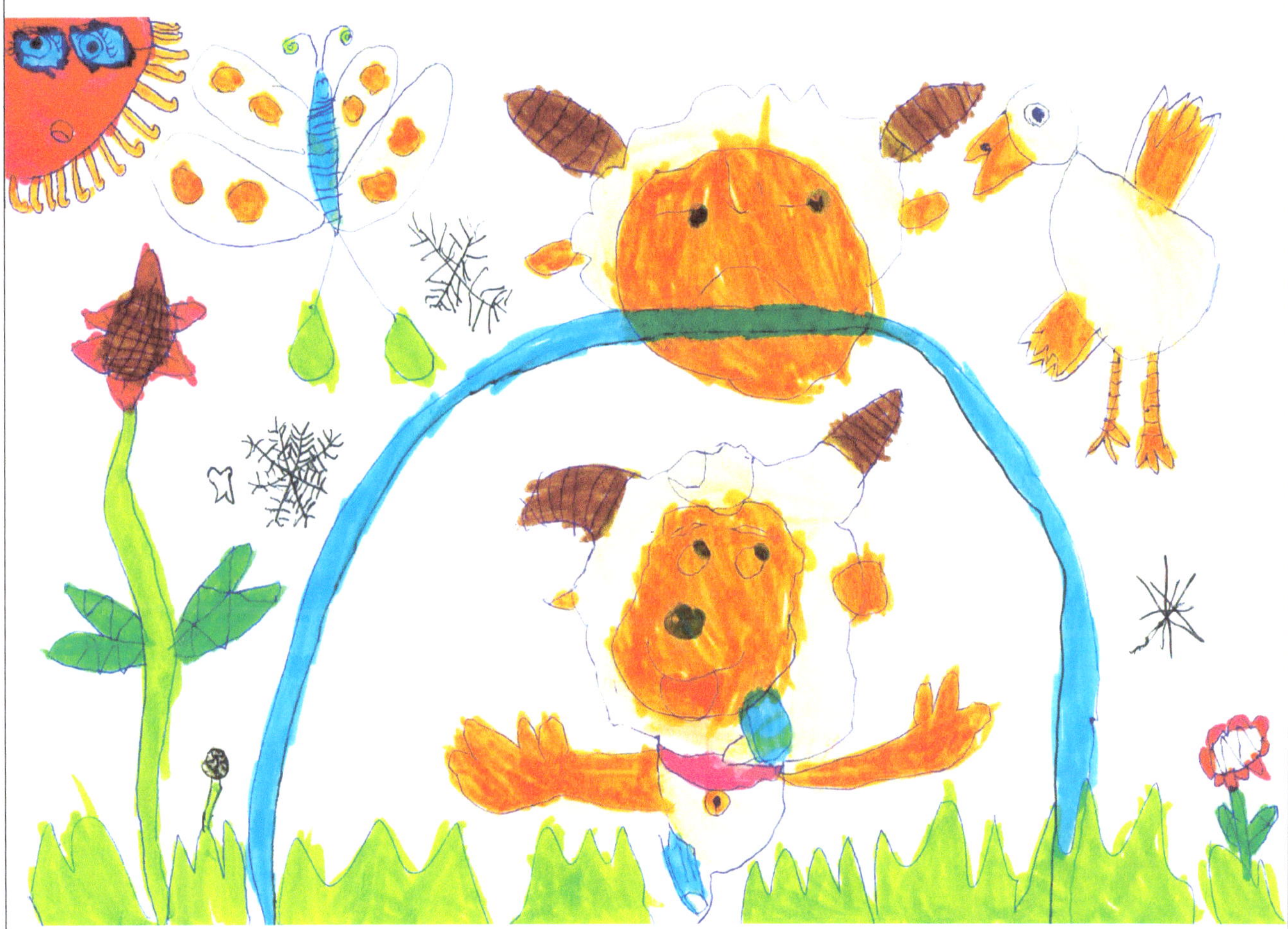

喜羊羊做操（The pleasant goat doing exercise）

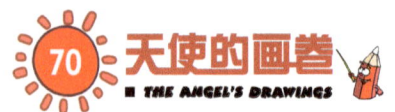

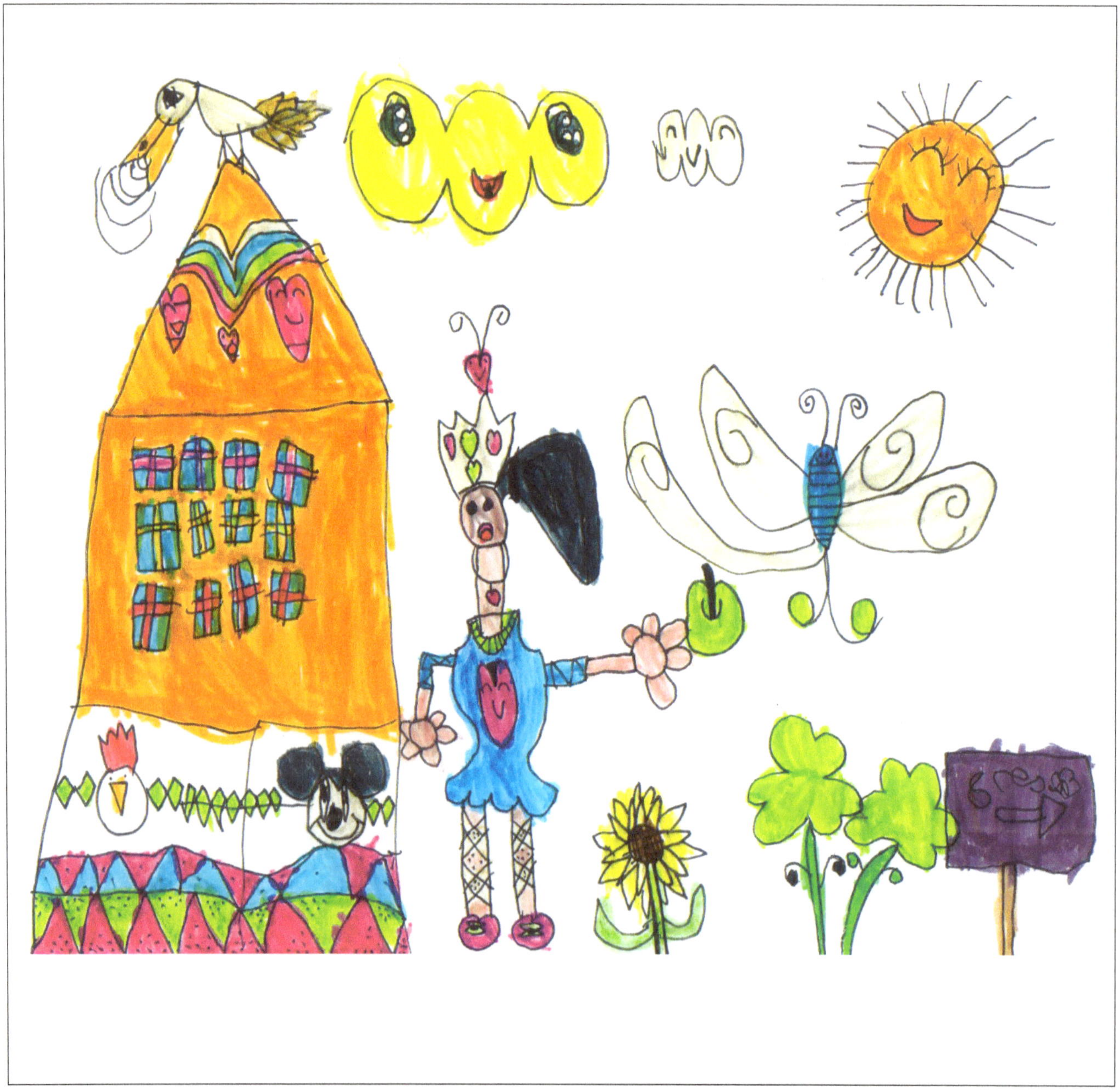

米妮给蝴蝶送苹果（Minnie giving an apple to the butterfly）

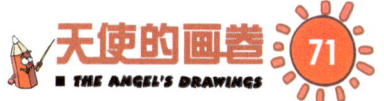

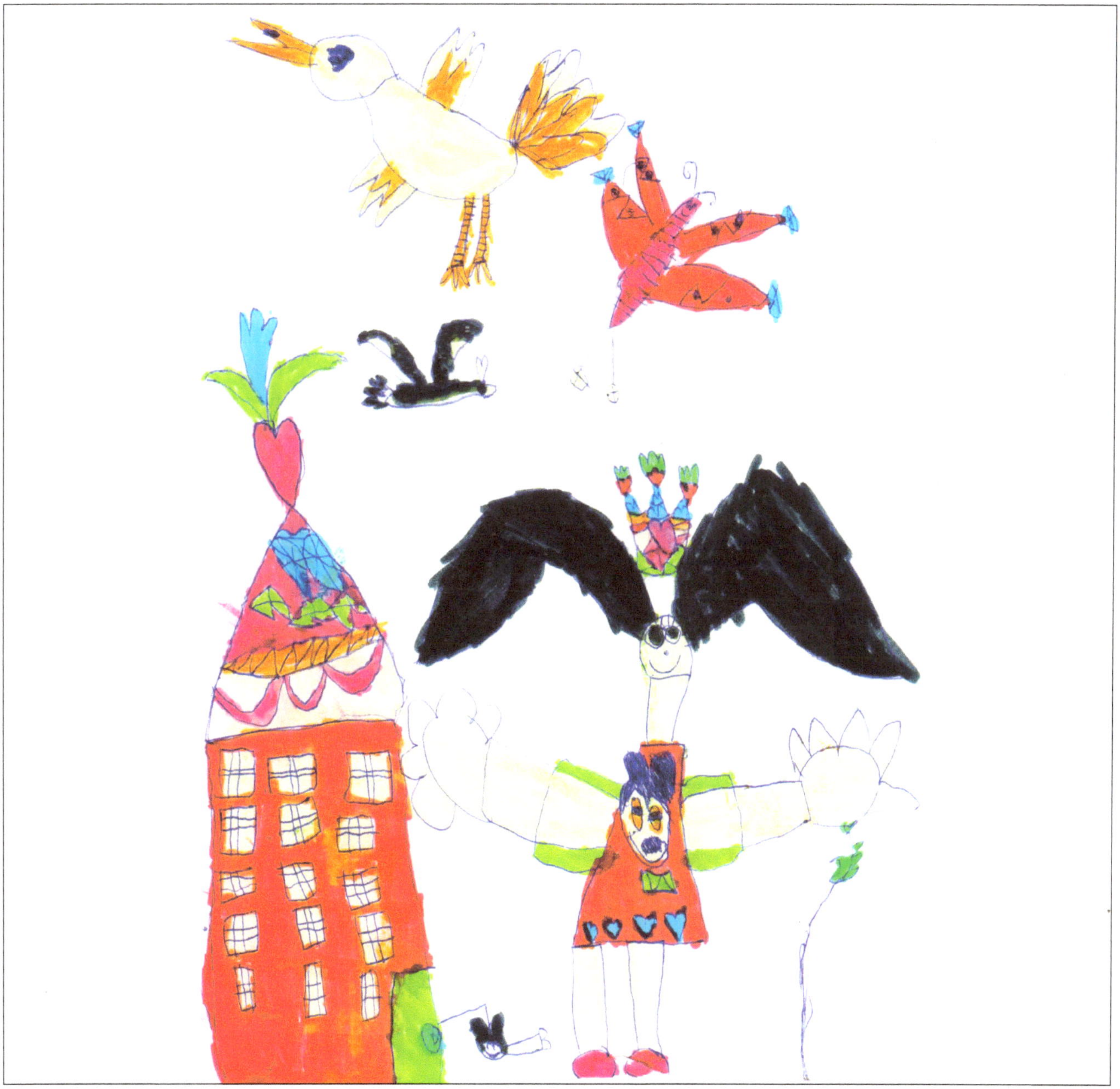

米妮照顾小动物（Minnie caring for little animals）

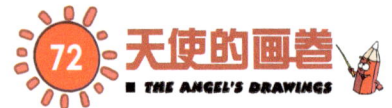

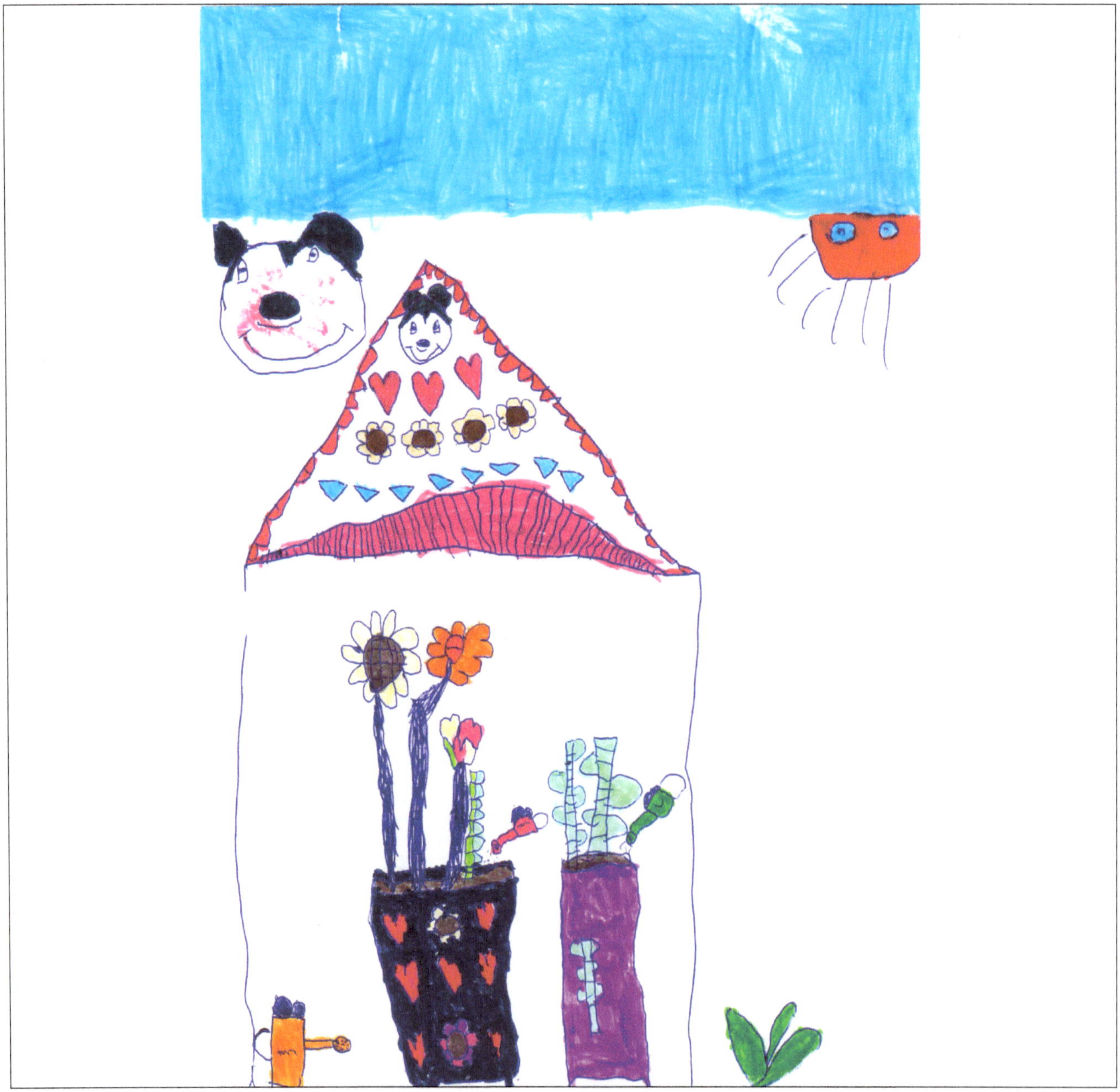

蓝天下的花房（The conservatory under the blue sky）

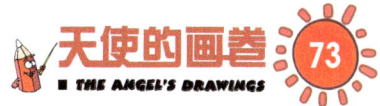

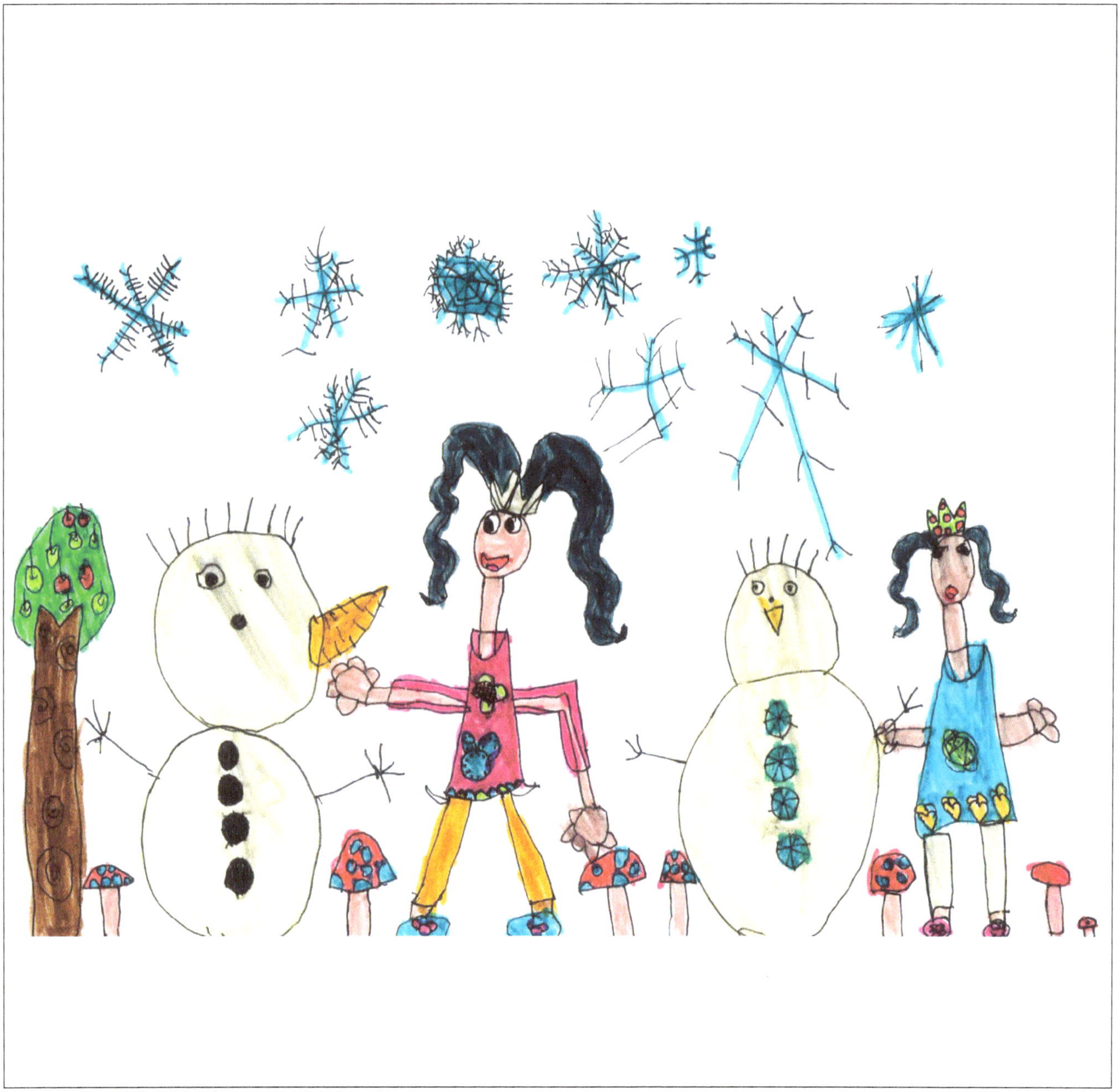

米奇和米妮堆雪人（Mickey and Minnie making snowmen）

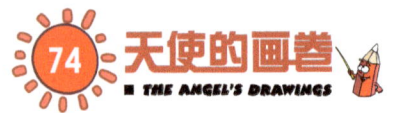

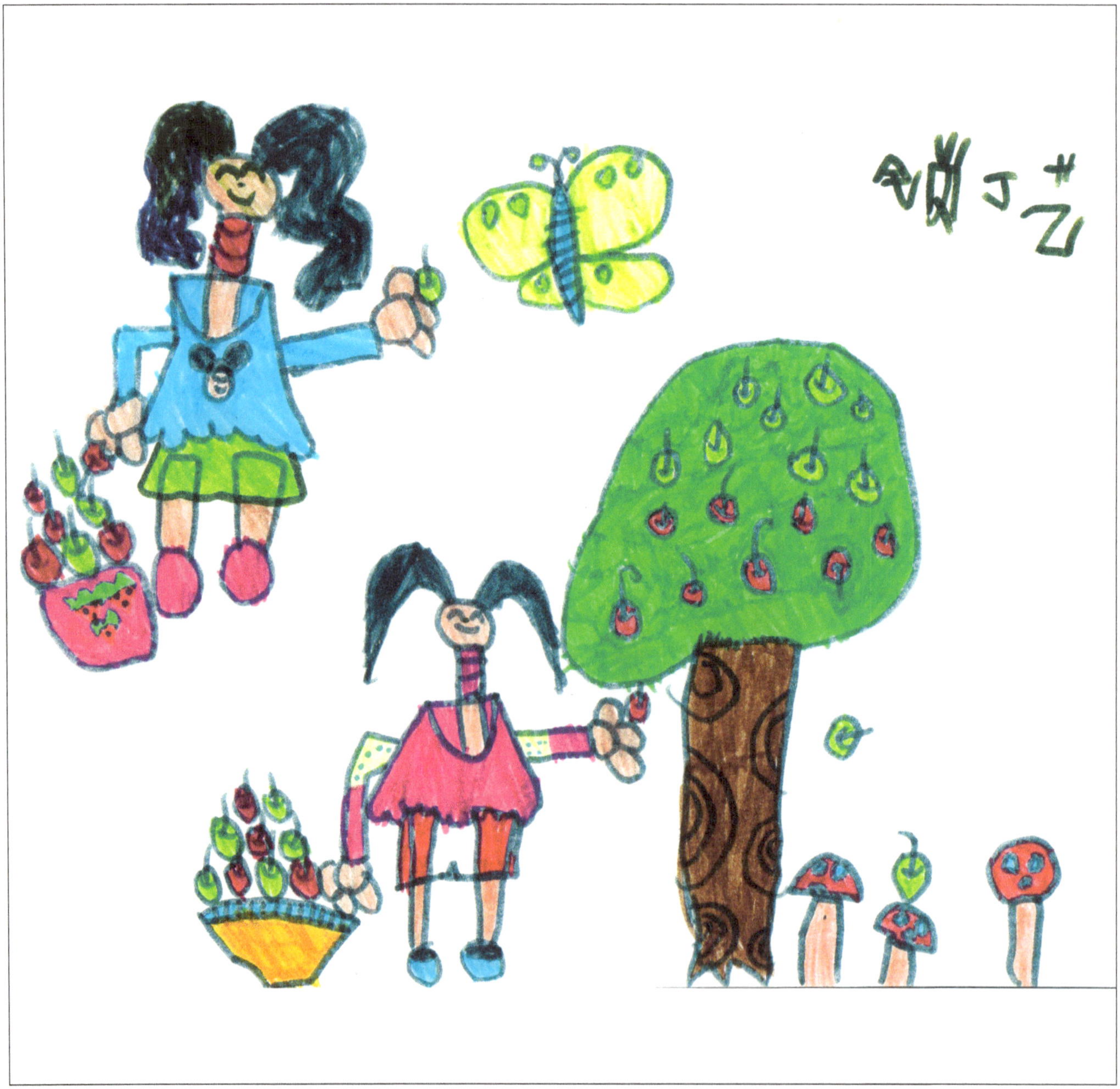

米奇和米妮摘苹果（Mickey and Minnie picking apples）